The Gift
of
Motherhood

Also by Chérie Carter-Scott, Ph.D.

If Success is a Game, These are the Rules

Is Love is a Game, These are the Rules

If Life is a Game, These are the Rules

If High School is a Game, Here's How to Break the Rules

Negaholics

The Corporate Negaholic

The New Species: The Evolution of the Human Being

The Inner View: A Woman's Daily Journal

Chicken Soup for the Global Soul®
(coauthored with Jack Canfield & Mark Victor Hansen) 2003

The Gift of Motherhood

10 Truths for Every Mother

Chérie Carter-Scott, Ph.D.

BROADWAY BOOKS / NEW YORK

PRINTED IN THE UNITED STATES OF AMERICA

Broadway Books titles may be purchased for business or promotional use or for special sales. For information, please write to: Special Markets Department, Random House, Inc., 1540 Broadway, New York, NY 10036.

BROADWAY BOOKS and its logo, a letter B bisected on the diagonal, are trademarks of Broadway Books, a division of Random House, Inc.

Visit our Web site at www.broadwaybooks.com

First edition published 2002

Designed by Donna Sinisgalli

Library of Congress Cataloging-in-Publication Data
Carter-Scott, Chérie.
The gift of motherhood : 10 truths for every mother /
Chérie Carter-Scott.
p. cm.
1. Motherhood. I. Title.
HQ759 .C29 2002
306.874'3—dc21
2001037579

ISBN 0-7679-04281

1 3 5 7 9 10 8 6 4 2

$\mathcal{W}$ith deep gratitude to all the women
who have "mothered" me:

Mary Kelly Untermeyer—biological mom
Barbara U. Carton-Ryker—sister-mom
Patricia Harris Walsh—surrogate mom
Margaret Darsie Carter—mother-in-love
Josie R. Pomije—mother-in-love
Lynn U. Stewart—co-parent

Acknowledgments

Karen Gallivan, Donna Gould, Maria Adams, Elizabeth Kleinveld, Linda Metzler, Josie Pomije, and the dozens of mothers who generously contributed their wisdom to this book.

Great thanks to Rachel Goldberg, who loves her mother, who "midwifed" this book, and who will one day be a wonderful mother.

Bob Barnett, my agent and representative, for whom I am dearly grateful.

Linda Michaels, who is the international godmother of this book. She ensures that people everywhere can reap the benefits.

Lauren Marino and Trish Medved, my editors, who have passed this book from one caretaker to another.

Debra Goldstein, who helped me articulate, define, recall, clarify, and listen to the guidance that wanted to be captured in this book.

I want to thank Lynn Stewart, Michael Pomije, stepdad; Bill Milham, godfather; Judy Rossiter, godmom; Susan Scott Miller; Russ Miller; Dorothea Scott; John Scott; Barbara Carton; Bob Steevensz; and extended family everywhere who supported me in mothering Jennifer, an experience that gave me the ultimate credentials to write this book.

Steve Rubin, who believes in the wisdom of the Game-Rules series of book.

Finally, I want to thank Jennifer Hayden Carter-Scott, who as my daughter enabled me to have the gift of motherhood.

Contents

Truth #4 :

CHILDREN BLOSSOM WHEN YOU
HONOR THEIR ESSENCE

Nurturing includes supporting what is unique and
special about them.   79

Truth #5 :

LOVE SHOWS UP IN MANY
DIFFERENT FORMS

Your specific expression of love will change
according to what your child
needs at the time.   106

Truth #6 :

AS YOUR CHILD GROWS, SO WILL YOU

Throughout your child's life, you will be presented with
opportunities to learn new lessons.   135

Truth #7 :

THERE WILL BE HIGHS AND LOWS

Amidst the challenges, there will be precious moments
that make it all worthwhile.   162

Truth #8 :

REMEMBERING TO CARE FOR
YOURSELF IS ESSENTIAL

Taking care of yourself enables you to take
better care of your child.   183

Introduction

Writing a book on motherhood has been an extremely challenging task; the only task that has been more challenging for me has been raising my daughter, Jennifer. It's difficult to put into words the experience of ushering a child into this world and being ultimately responsible for her care, well-being, and development. It is an incredibly overwhelming, astounding, and miraculous experience that almost defies description.

Volumes have been written about motherhood—what it entails, what is required, what it provides, and thoughts on how to do it "correctly." I'm not necessarily an expert on all these concerns, but after decades of coaching and counseling many thousands of women worldwide I have learned some basic universal truths associated with this experience. Knowing these truths in advance—or along the way—doesn't guarantee absolute success, but it certainly will make the journey easier.

Though we all have common concerns, wishes, hopes, and fears, no two experiences of motherhood are identical. Every child is unique, and every mother has her own path to walk. I raised a daughter with the help of my sister and later my husband, but often it seemed like it was solely on my own, where others have a spouse or partner. Some women are blessed with financial security and are free from concern about their survival; others must struggle to ensure that they and their children are clothed and fed. Some have children who are gifted, bright, or well behaved, while others must address continuous discipline, learning issues, or disabilities.

When I became pregnant, I was filled with new thoughts and feelings. I, of course, wanted to be the "perfect" mother, but I also felt there were many gaps in my experience and feared that I might fall short of the mark. I took the responsibility very seriously and wanted to create a world of safety, encouragement, opportunity, and unconditional love for my child. I wanted to provide a kind of human greenhouse where my child could grow in the healthiest, most positive and fulfilling manner. I took courses to prepare myself, and set out on the journey to become the perfect mother.

Little did I know that having Jennifer would bring increased stress to my marriage. Rather than an environment of tranquil harmony, there was friction. When she was 18 months old, her father left us. I had never anticipated being both mother and father to my child. If I had felt slightly insecure as a mother, I now felt totally inadequate as a nurturer/breadwinner. She was a child who required one-on-one attention and needed constant reassurance. She was everything my mother had wished on me . . . to have a child just like me.

All women have their own ideas about how to raise children. What worked for me may not work for you, and what works for you may not work for your circle of friends. Trial and error, intuition and "how to" coaching, taking charge and letting go all contribute to learning the lessons of motherhood. Underneath it all, the ten truths in this book stand out as universal for every mother, regardless of her circumstances, nationality, race, or religion.

Keep these truths as gentle reminders on your journey. There are no hard-and-fast rules you must obey, no detailed programs to follow. Choose the methods that resonate with you. More than anything, these truths will provide you with a road map that you can refer to when life seems overwhelming or you lose your way.

Motherhood is many things to many women: a journey, an adventure, a job, a calling, a responsibility, an opportunity, and a gift. For some it brings more joy, for others, endless challenges. It's different for every woman. The underlying truths are presented here so you can find comfort when the task seems too big, find light when the road is too dark, and find handrails when you feel like you need support. Remember that like all the women who have gone before you, you are up to the task, and you have the ability to fulfill your vision of becoming the best mother you can be.

Everything about the experience of being a mother stretched me. I had to find resources within myself that I didn't know I had. I had to learn patience at a deeper level than I'd ever known. I had to let go of my way of doing things and let my daughter find her own way. I had to learn how to connect, how to engage and calm her when I felt like nothing I could do would work. It has been like graduate school in the world of human development. She has taught me humility, forgiveness, unattachment, joy, and boundless love.

Recently my daughter Jennifer wrote me this letter.

It is the end of the year 2000, and I look at those who have been there for me. You are the first to come to mind. You are my rock, by my side encouraging me and knowing that I will make it through. Some people believe that they have a guardian angel that watches over them and does small things to help them along their path through life. My guardian angel is more apparent and more hands-on, and she makes sure that whatever I do, I do it knowing what I'm getting into. You are my guardian angel. You are my mother. I want to thank you for all that you do, all that you share with me, and all that you give to me . . . you are my inspiration and I thank you.

Love always,
Jennifer

I share this letter with you because despite my concerns, fears, and feelings of insecurity, she has blossomed into a strong, smart, kind, resourceful, and beautiful woman. I wasn't the perfect mother, but I did the best I could, and that's all any child can ask.

Blessings on your journey,
Chérie Carter-Scott, Ph.D.

Truth #1

HAVING A CHILD
CHANGES YOUR LIFE

Your reality is transformed the moment your child arrives.

Welcome to motherhood: the single most profound and transformative rite of passage a woman can experience. Of course, there are other major turning points throughout our lives—puberty, graduations, career achievements, marriage—but none can really compare to the experience of welcoming a child into this world and being responsible for its care. Motherhood is the most precious gift as well as the ultimate responsibility . . . and the doorway to the most extraordinary love you have ever known. It stretches you beyond what you ever imagined you were capable of. It can be a source of supreme fulfillment and, at times, a source of some of the deepest heartbreak.

To say that motherhood transforms your life forever is something of an understatement. The moment your child is born, your life undergoes seismic changes; however things were before this tiny creature arrived, they certainly are no longer that way. It turns your life, your schedule, your perspective, and your relationships inside out, backward, and upside down. You feel a love that is different from anything you've ever felt before. What mattered before seems less significant as a whole new set of priorities arise, and you experience life in a totally new way. When you assume the new identity of "mother," within an instant your world is never quite the same again.

It's difficult to anticipate what will be on the other side of the changes, or what your life will look like after a baby arrives. You can plan, prepare, speculate, and imagine, but what it comes down to is this: no one knows exactly how their life will change when they become a parent. They only know for certain that it will.

So many women I've counseled over the years express real fear at the magnitude of the changes a baby can bring. While most of them were thrilled at the idea of becoming a mother—something many of them had dreamt about for years—there were still twinges of fear or even panic when they thought about how much their lives were about to change. One client described it as "nine months on the diving board, not quite knowing what you're about to plunge into."

On the flip side of fear lies excitement—even exhilaration. There is the spiritual sense that you are making a contribution to the eternal circle of life, that you are joining the ranks of an honored sisterhood. You are crossing a threshold in your life, and you will now be able to give all you know to another living being. There is anticipation of the rewards: the sweet kisses, the warmth of a grateful hug, precious finger paintings and the glitter Mother's Day cards, the pride of seeing them make strides both big and small. My friend Laura swears she could make millions if she could just bottle and sell the expression of pure delight on her three-year-old's face when she searches and finds her mother among all the other moms waiting outside nursery school. That moment alone makes all the upheaval and change worth it.

Motherhood opens the door to a whole new range of experiences. Whether you approach it with trepidation or excitement, it will change your life in more ways than you can imagine.

The Rhythm of Your Life

When a child enters the world through you, it alters everything on a psychic, psychological, and purely practical level.   JANE FONDA

Each of us has a rhythm to our lives. It's the framework we set for the notes we play out each and every day. Whether you are conscious of it or not, you have a specific rhythm to the way you presently live your life. It's what makes you comfortable, and it comprises all the patterns to which you and your mate have become accustomed. You know when and how you take your coffee or tea, what you will do on Saturday night, which movies you plan to see, how much time it takes you to complete your workout. Hopefully, your life runs smoothly most of the time as all the parts flow together in harmony. Then along comes baby, and suddenly none of them flow quite the same way anymore.

It's hard to describe how radically life changes when you bring a new baby into the mix. Amy was among the first in her group of friends to have a baby, and whenever she was with her friends she was keenly aware of how different her life was from before. She and her husband, Phil, used to go out at least once every weekend with their friends to dinner or a movie, yet once Zach was born, it wasn't quite so easy. There were baby-sitting arrangements to be made, cellular phones to be left on in case of an emergency, and they got tired much earlier in the evening (due to the fact that they had been up the whole night before with Zach). Their friends would order a few drinks with dinner, but Amy refrained because she was nursing. Amy's friends would talk about going to a spa for a girls' weekend, and she knew she wouldn't feel comfortable leaving Zach until he was a little older. Amy and Phil began to notice more and more that they had entered a new life phase, and that the way they had run their lives before would need to evolve.

The first few months with a newborn are when the changes are most apparent. That time can be something akin to spiritual ecstasy and logistical chaos. There is nursing and/or bottles to be made, cries to calm, diapers to be changed, lullabies to sing in hopes of putting the little one back to sleep at 3 A.M. There is an endless array of stuff: blankets, strollers, pacifiers, and toys everywhere. As your child grows, suddenly your schedule is filled with play dates, doctor appointments, and swim and tumbling classes, as you and your partner try to juggle all this new baby activity with all the grown-up parts of your life. Where before your bag may have held your lipstick, keys, credit card, and Palm Pilot, now it is bulging with diapers, wipes, pacifiers, and bottles. *The Practice* is replaced by *Sesame Street*; sushi is eclipsed by mashed bananas; "dry clean only" is traded in for wash-

and-wear. You can't even name the latest movie, let alone see it, and you probably haven't thought about sex or romance in ages. You may not even recognize the life you are presently living, and you're not sure how things changed so radically so fast.

Almost every mother I've spoken to has had an experience that somewhat resembles this scenario. I had a newborn almost twenty years ago, and although some specific elements have changed, the general idea is still basically the same. Although some fortunate mothers experience a very smooth transition from being childless to having their firstborn, the majority of women I know experience significant upheaval. No matter how hard we try to convince ourselves that we are different, it's impossible for our lives to go on as usual right after the baby is born.

Becky was an organized, efficient woman with a demanding job in marketing. She and her husband waited until they were both 36 to have their first baby, so Becky felt she was prepared. Since she was very accustomed to masterminding large projects in her work, she assumed she could handle her new role as a mother in much the same way. Many months after the fact, she admitted she had secretly believed she would be able to give birth and incorporate her baby into her life as it was. She would simply take the baby in stride. During her pregnancy, she organized in advance: made lists, ordered furniture, did all the "required" reading, and made arrangements with her office for how things were to be handled while she was on maternity leave. She prepared well and felt confident that it would all go according to plan.

The problem was that newborns don't tend to fit into preset

agendas. (Talk to any woman with a child and she'll confirm that!) It wasn't as easy as she'd imagined to just fold the baby into her schedule. Becky planned to work from home every day from one to three, but her new daughter, Brooke, had no intention of taking a nap when Mom had planned for it. Whenever Becky was on an important phone call, Brooke would start to cry. When she tried to pack up Brooke's things to get the two of them out the door on time to make a lunch appointment, Brooke promptly threw up all over everything, and they had to go back inside and start over. Becky and her husband had agreed in advance that they would take turns going to the gym in the morning, a routine that was important to both of them, but they were both often too exhausted to even consider exercising. Even their plans to continue their Saturday morning ritual of picking up coffee and taking it to the park by the river were interrupted because the only thing that would satisfy their baby in the mornings was watching a video.

"I definitely thought I had it all figured out," Becky told me, laughing. "It was all going to go according to how I planned. I figured that if I was organized enough it would be easy. The strange thing is that the more in control you think you are, the more challenging it is to adapt."

Becky's problem was that she was resisting the new rhythm of her life. She was rigidly clinging to the way things used to be (and the way she envisioned they "should be"), and as a result, was frustrated and depleted most of the time. Her life wasn't running according to plan. The dance had changed, and she was out of step.

I interviewed many women as I was writing this book, and when

I asked them what changed about their lives when they became mothers, almost all of them mentioned the loss of absolute control over how they allocated their time and energy. Where before they were accustomed to arranging their lives around what they and their partner wanted, now they were at the mercy of a larger force in a smaller package that required them to yield to its wants and needs.

After my daughter Jennifer was born, I was most surprised by the fact that what I did every day had to change. Before she was born, I organized my days around "what needed to be done and what I wanted to do." Suddenly, the way I spent my time was no longer determined by my wishes and desires. Instead, it was now dictated by Jennifer's timetable and requirements. If she was hungry, it was mealtime, no matter where we were. If she was cranky, it was lullaby time. If she wanted attention, it was playtime. And so it went. It took me awhile to adjust to this shift, since up until that point I hadn't really been accountable to anyone except my mate, my clients, and myself. Of course, the demands changed as Jennifer grew, but those first few months were a real challenge.

There is a popular myth that the maternal instinct will enable you to handle all this with grace and ease—that the bliss of a newborn eclipses all the chaos and fears. Yet talk to any woman who is in the midst of those first few months, and she will tell you it is hard work! You don't just snap your fingers and effortlessly glide into the role of "mother." Beyond all there is to learn and do, there is a tremendous adjustment that must be made. Just like all other life stages that came before, it takes time and patience to learn the new rhythms of this one. Learning to deal with all the changes is the first step.

DEALING WITH THE CHANGES

What I discovered, and what many other women like Becky discovered, was that ultimately, the best way to deal with the sudden changes in your life and your routines when your baby comes along is to simply go with them. You can be in control up to a point, but flexibility is the key to surviving the first few months with a newborn. Preparation is always beneficial, but that's only what happens *before* the baby arrives; once you're in the thick of it, what's really needed is willingness to surrender to what is.

Motherhood is the ultimate opportunity to learn the lesson of surrender. The more rigid you are, the harder the process is. The more you try to will things to go certain ways, the more frustrated you may become. On the other hand, the more you're willing to go with the flow, the more harmonious your experience will be. When you relax into the situation, you may find new ways of being and coping that are available to you that you haven't considered before. Allowing for spontaneity invites the little miracles to happen. First steps can't be planned. You may miss the cooing sounds of your baby's giggle, or the delicious scent of her clean body after bathtime, or the peaceful look on your angel's face as she lies there fast asleep if you are too busy trying to organize things or make them run according to plan. The moments that matter rarely happen according to anyone's preset agenda.

It may take a little time, but every mother eventually creates new routines that work for her. Making the shift from being on your own or part of a couple to becoming a family isn't easy, but it can be done—and has been done millions of times before. You've transitioned before in your lifetime, and all your skills will come into play here. Trust yourself. Let go of your idea of how it was "supposed to be." Ask for guidance from other mothers whom you respect. Rely on those around you who are willing to help out, especially your partner. Relax, breathe, trust; you'll find your new rhythm in time.

A Shift in Perspective

When people ask me what I do, I always say I am a mother first. Your children represent your thoughts. Your children are a statement.

JACQUELINE JACKSON

"Motherhood made me focus on someone else rather than myself," explains Alison, a 33-year-old mother. "It's not that I was necessarily selfish before, just more self-concerned. All decisions I made regarding my life centered around my husband and me, but every decision I make now revolves around our baby."

Alison summed up well the shift in perspective that happens when we become mothers. Whereas before we had been focused on ourselves—which is a normal and healthy way to be—now our focus shifts to a being outside ourselves. This affects everything, from what's important to us to how we spend our money to what we worry about. It can affect our views, our opinions, and even our values.

For Trish, the shift showed up in terms of worrying about her appearance. Trish was never quite happy with the way she looked—

she didn't like her hair color, tried again and again to lose that last ten pounds, and could never quite find anything to wear that she felt great in. Of course, a great deal of this was in her mind (her friends said she was lovely), but Trish didn't agree and as a result put a lot of energy into working on her appearance. When her daughter Emily was born, Trish suddenly had other things to focus on besides her reflection in the mirror. It wasn't until Emily was six months old that Trish realized her preoccupation with looking perfect had waned. It wasn't that she let herself go and became frumpy; far from it. The irony was that Trish still looked terrific—but what occupied her thoughts was something other than how she looked.

Susan, on the other hand, noticed a shift in the way she conducted her financial life. She and her husband, Brian, liked the good life and frequently lived beyond their means. It was common for their bank balance to dip into the red at the end of each month. They both had good jobs, but somehow their combined salaries seemed to slip out of their fingers too easily, leaving nothing left for savings. When Susan received a bonus from her company at the end of the year, they immediately booked an island vacation. When Brian got a raise, the extra money was swallowed up by their monthly bills.

After the birth of their son, Susan started to feel panicky about not having any money saved. She started to think about things like the cost of summer camp and swimming lessons, and escalating college costs. She slowly stopped buying things on impulse and tried to make do with the clothes and other things she already had. She encouraged Brian to cut back as well, so they could set some money aside each month. They still live quite well, but now they are both more conscious of where their money goes. They have already earmarked Susan's bonus this year as the start of their son's college fund.

Lori noticed a change in her willingness to take risks. She had always loved excitement, and before they had their two kids she and her husband, Stu, spent their free time skiing black diamond runs, rock climbing, river rafting, and trying out other kinds of extreme sports. Lori was always the one who said "yes" to any kind of spontaneous adventure. After their first son was born, Lori and Stu assumed they would return to the sports they loved. Yet each time Stu suggested they arrange for a climb or go skiing, Lori invented some reason not to go. She kept saying they would go next week, next month, next year. On the surface, it sounded like Lori was too preoccupied with the baby to enjoy herself, but upon looking a little deeper, she discovered that the underlying reason was a core concern for their physical safety. A serious accident would not only impact them, it would affect their son's entire future.

Lori's life had changed. She had changed. Her choices had changed. She realized that her son's well-being would be impacted by every decision she made. Lori eventually found a happy balance. She knew she couldn't go back to being entirely carefree, but she also didn't want to give up an important part of her life that she enjoyed. She revealed her concerns to Stu, and together they decided to find new activities that would satisfy their yearnings for adventure with less risk. Now they climb mountains that are less steep and ski runs that are less extreme but that still provide the adventure they seek.

Simone noticed that she became much more playful once her twins Annie and Tammy were born. She had always been fairly reserved, yet when her girls started to smile and crawl, she got down on the floor and joined in with them. She sang goofy songs to make them laugh, and laughed when she got baby food in her hair. Becoming a mother lightened her up and allowed her to play.

You may be surprised at the effect your child has on you. It's difficult to anticipate how your views will change when you become a mother. You may be determined to never impose limits on your child, until the moment he or she scribbles on the living room wall with magic marker. You may insist that you will not stop working, until spending time with your child becomes the most precious thing imaginable. You might believe that your political views are set in stone, until you measure the impact that those views will have on your child's future. The most important lesson is to never say "never," since we don't really know how we will change until we get there.

THE IDENTITY ISSUE

Motherhood may force you to find a new way to define yourself. This is particularly true for women with careers. If you have forged a path for yourself that involves advancing toward career goals, you may be faced with one of the most controversial dilemmas of women today: how to balance career and motherhood. This is a dilemma not only in terms of how to work out the logistics of child care, but also in terms of how you as an individual appear in the world.

As a society, we have come a fairly long way in terms of opportunities for women. There is plenty of room for discussion about that, and it isn't necessarily the reality around the world. However, it is possible for women to not only work, but to create careers as well.

There are women in powerful positions in industries including politics, manufacturing, finance, technology, literature, engineering, and aviation. No matter how accomplished a woman may be, however, she will need to face the identity issues that will arise if she decides to become a mother.

How do you balance career demands and the desire to be with your baby? How do you define yourself when you feel split, with one finger sending an important fax and one pressing "play" on an animated video? How do you decide whether to go back to work full-time, to take a part-time job, to start a new career that gives you more flexibility, or to become a full-time stay-at-home mother, if that is a financial option? These are only some of the questions that arise. Even today, when many fathers are involved in sharing parenting responsibilities, and some even stay at home with the children, women still need to address these options. If they have the financial flexibility to not work, they will be faced with a major life choice that can be difficult to make.

Kimberly loved her job as an assistant curator at a museum. She had studied art for many years and worked long, hard hours to get to where she was. While many of her friends were having children, Kimberly dedicated her energy to achieving her career goals. She was highly respected in her field, and it was assumed she would take over as curator when the person in that position retired.

Kimberly's identity was very much wrapped up in what she did for a living. When she had first moved to her city, she knew only a handful of people, and it was through her job that she became part of a wide social circle. She was by nature quite shy, and her career status boosted her self-confidence. Her job provided an entrée into an exciting world filled with talented, well-known artists whom she admired. Her job at the museum elevated her to professional status that she felt good about, and she enjoyed knowing she was having an impact on the cultural awareness of thousands of people.

When she became pregnant, she had every intention of returning to work full-time, which she did four months after her son, Jason, was born. Kimberly and her husband were able to afford a good nanny to watch Jason during the day, and she believed it was all falling into place nicely.

Yet returning to work was far more difficult than Kimberly had anticipated. She assumed that since she dearly loved her work, returning to her job would not present the same dilemma that it did for many other women. Yet that wasn't the case. With each passing day, Kimberly felt a yearning to be with her son. Every time she caught sight of his tiny face in the photo on her desk, her heart sank a little. She called home often to hear what Jason was doing at that moment. When she should have been concentrating on a new exhibit, her thoughts drifted to Jason. On a daily basis, Kimberly felt torn between her career and her son.

Finally, she went to her director to ask if she could work out a part-time arrangement, or if there was a way she could bring Jason to work two days a week. Unfortunately, the answer was "no" to both requests, and Kimberly was faced with a tough choice. Should she stay at the job that she had worked so hard to get, or seize the moment to be with her child before he entered school?

Ultimately, Kimberly left her position at the museum. She and her husband were fortunate enough to be able to live on his income alone, and Kimberly became a full-time mother—a shift that was very difficult for her. Though she was thrilled to be the primary caretaker of their son, she was also left a bit confused about how to define herself without her job. She was no longer "Kimberly, assistant curator." Now she was "Kimberly, Jason's mom," which sounded less prestigious to her. She hadn't been aware of how much she defined herself in terms of her job, and suddenly she had to redefine herself once again.

Kimberly eventually embraced her new role as full-time mother. Though she felt a twinge when she read about the opening of an exhibit that she had worked on, she still wouldn't have traded that opening for the excitement she felt when Jason grasped the edge of the coffee table and hoisted himself upright for the first time. When he puts his arms around her neck every night and lays his head on her shoulder, saying their special goodnight, "I love you all the way to the moon and back," Kimberly knows in her heart that she made the right choice.

Hope's story is different. Three months to the day after her daughter was born, Hope went back to her job at a high-tech company. Though she loved her daughter, Hope found herself craving contact with the adult world. After the chaos of the first three months, she actually looked forward to Monday mornings and the order of her work life. At first, Hope felt guilty about missing her job. Shouldn't her maternal instinct make her want to be home with her baby? Was she being selfish by caring so much about work? Shouldn't her daughter be her number-one concern?

Hope came to talk to me to sort out these concerns. Her mother was pressuring her to quit her job and stay home with April, the implication was that that was what good mothers did. Her best friend, who was very career-oriented, encouraged her to go back, claiming she would become "boring" if she stayed home all day with a baby. Her life partner hoped that she would choose to be a stay-at-home mom, but said he understood and would support her if she chose not to. As we talked, Hope began to see that she hadn't even had the chance to think about what she really wanted amidst all the opinions of those around her. When she became still and listened to her own message within, she saw clearly that her dedication to work and to her daughter did not need to be mutually exclusive. She knew she wanted to work during the weekdays, and spend her evenings and weekends with her family. While this might not suit everyone's needs, it was the scenario that worked best for Hope.

Many people will feel they have every right to impose upon you their viewpoint on how you should raise your child. If you choose to walk the path of a mother who works, you can be certain there will be those who raise their eyebrows in disapproval. On the one hand, society cheers for women who succeed, but on the other hand, it condemns women who are not dedicated exclusively to their children. Hopefully, the world will continue to evolve so that these issues become less stressful. In the meantime, however, only you can assess what is ultimately right for you and your family. Others may try to persuade you that their way is right or best, but just as with any other personal decision, it's essential that you make this choice based on what you and your partner want, not on what the rest of the world thinks you should do. After all, it's your baby, and your life.

If this is a dilemma that you are facing, it might help to consider the following questions as you process your choice:

When I consider going back to work, how do I feel?
When I consider staying home with my child, what feelings arise?
What is my biggest concern about going back to work?
What is my biggest concern about being a stay-at-home mom?
Are there creative solutions to address these concerns?
Are there compromises available to me (i.e., working part-time, working from home, starting a freelance business that allows me to work from home, etc.)?
Is there anyone who has created a work/child-care scenario that I admire, and from which I can learn?

Answering these questions may not lead you directly to the solution, but they will put you in touch with what is true for you. Making a choice such as this certainly isn't easy, but you have a far greater chance of making the one that is authentic for you if you are honest with yourself and your partner about your needs and desires.

Impact on Your Relationship

When you have a baby, you set off an explosion in your marriage, and when the dust settles, your marriage is different from what it was. Not better, necessarily; not worse, necessarily; but different.   NORA EPHRON

One plus one makes three. You and your partner were a unit before your baby arrived, and now that unit has been expanded. It has metamorphosed into something else. You are now a family.

When you and your spouse become parents, your dynamic as a couple will change. At best, it can bring you two closer together. There is something truly awe-inspiring about creating a being from your combined flesh and blood that is impossible to describe. You look into the face of this tiny creature who was formed by the linking of your DNA, and you experience a whole new level of union. You begin a new journey of co-creation as you work together to shape, guide, and protect this new person.

Judy and Mike felt a new appreciation for each other when they became parents. For Judy, it was a chance to experience Mike's tender side. It made her feel so good to see her six-foot-two-inch, 200-pound husband picking up their tiny son and singing "The Itsy-Bitsy Spider." Mike loved watching Judy's creativity come alive as she invented clever ways to get their son to eat his carrots. Being parents brought out wonderful traits in both of them, and they say it drew them closer together.

That's not to say there weren't any tensions; no family dynamic is absolutely perfect. There were times when they felt stressed and frustrated, but that's normal. Overall, though, Judy and Mike rate parenthood as a positive experience for their relationship.

When your baby enters your world, you will create a triangle, with one point requiring more attention, time, and energy than the other two. Whether the reaction is instant familial bliss, stress, or a constant interplay between the two, there is a definite shift in the dynamic of your lives together. Previously, you may both have been comfortable with the energy you received from each other; now you have another being in your midst who wants and needs to be in the center.

My friend Donna recently told me this story. She and her husband, Seth, were at the diner with their two children, ages three and six. Donna was trying to tell Seth something important that happened at work that day, and Seth was trying to listen to what she was saying and give her feedback about it. However, their kids had other ideas. It went something like this:

> Donna: I couldn't believe my boss said that to me, can you? . . . Devon, take that out of your mouth. It's dirty.
> Seth: So what did you say to him? . . . Waitress, may I please have more napkins? We spilled some juice over here!
> Donna: I tried, but he . . . oops, can you reach Devon's bunny? It fell under the table. Devon, hang on, Daddy's getting your bunny . . .

Seth (from under the table): Where is it . . . oh, I've got it. So, now, what did you tell him?

Humorous, yes, but this is just a snippet of what life can sometimes look like when you become parents. Thankfully, Donna and Seth's marriage has a strong foundation, and they take pains to ensure it stays that way.

The connection between you and your partner can be easily eroded or eclipsed in the course of raising your family. There are many demands that require your attention and pull you in all directions. Your focus may be so divided that tending to the nurturing and care of your relationship may fall by the wayside. It may happen without you being aware of it. I have counseled many couples who lavished all their time and attention on their children only to find themselves living with someone who is merely a roommate once their children are grown and gone.

In the movie *The Story of Us,* Michelle Pfeiffer and Bruce Willis play a couple who are intensely devoted to their children, and whose marriage falls apart as they negotiate the challenging years of parenthood. There is one particularly poignant scene in which Michelle Pfeiffer's character remarks that, as a couple, you can get by year after year without ever actually looking at each other. When both people are facing outward toward their children all the time, eye contact—and every other kind of connection between them—may get lost. They videotape first steps, cheer at soccer games, but never remember to actually turn and face each other.

Staying connected to each other as more than just parents is important not only for the sake of your relationship, but also for your children. Your children witness your relationship, and from it they learn how to relate to their own mates. Your dynamic as a couple is the primary model from which they draw their expectations. This is a pretty tall order, but it's another powerful reason why it is so important to care for your relationship.

STAYING CONNECTED

It is up to you and your spouse to find deliberate ways to stay connected in order to keep from becoming co-parents who are merely housemates. You may need to find some creativity in light of the multiplying demands for your time and attention, but your efforts will be well worth it. The stronger your connection with your mate, the better parents you will be. The happier you are in the context of your primary relationship, the more love and joy you will have available to give to your children. Love needs to be refueled, and you and your spouse are the best sources of energy and affection for each other.

Here are a few creative ways some couples maintain their connection:

1. Search for "alone time together." Plan weekends away, or if that isn't possible, find an hour here or there. One couple mentioned that their newborn usually slept between the hours of 6 and 9 A.M., so they would set the alarm to be able to spend those hours together.

2. If you can, schedule a weekly "date night." Use any resources

you have—baby-sitters, an au pair, parents or in-laws, or even friends with whom you can trade baby-sitting services. Be religious about honoring your date night.

3. Have at least one conversation each day that is not about the children, even if it is only for five minutes. "How are *you*?" is a question that may prompt this.

4. Stay involved in adult activities together. Certainly, Saturdays at the playground or zoo can be fun, but it's helpful to also stay connected to what you loved together as grown-ups. If you used to go to the theater together, make efforts to do that once in awhile. Make plans with adult friends to go out to dinner without the baby. See a new movie that *isn't* animated.

5. Use technology. One couple sends e-mails back and forth daily as a way to keep up with each other and have little private exchanges.

6. Keep your sex life alive, no matter what it takes. Be as creative as you can, but pay attention to this. Making love can help keep your connection alive!

Come up with whatever ways you can think of to stay connected. Whatever is unique about your relationship, remember to honor it. Whatever drew you together in the first place, revisit it often. Whatever keeps you in sync with each other, do it. Find the time and the energy to do these things, even when it seems impossible. In the long run, you'll be glad you did.

NEGOTIATING RESPONSIBILITIES

If you and your partner are raising your children together, there will always be times when you need to negotiate who does what. There is a lot to be done when it comes to raising children. There are the logistics: who gets up for feedings, who takes care of diapers, baths, and sore throats, who provides laughter, and who picks your child up from day care or school. There is the emotional aspect: who wipes away the tears, who patches the boo-boos, who cheers them on daily. There is also the guidance factor: who teaches them how to say their ABCs, how to hold a fork or use a tissue, who teaches them not to talk to strangers, and who disciplines them when they misbehave. And that's just the beginning!

The old-fashioned way of raising children involved the mother basically doing it all, and the father arriving home after a long day at work to say a quick "good night." But family dynamics have changed with the times. There are no givens anymore, no automatic ways of structuring roles, no absolute rules for delegating responsibilities. It's all up to us, and it's all about creating systems that work for you.

Certain roles or responsibilities may automatically fall to each person, based on what they are good at. For example, Betsy handles the family finances, so it is she who determines their children's allowances. Her husband, Bob, is handy, so science projects are his domain. Betsy is a book editor, so she tends to read the bedtime stories. Bob likes sports, so he's the one who taught their children to ride bikes and how to hit a baseball. As a couple, they had little problem delegating the tasks that came naturally to each of them.

Where cloudiness can arise is in the areas that no one automatically "claims." Both were squeamish about blood, so who would bandage the injuries? Both had demanding jobs, so who would take off from work for a school event? Neither liked to cook, so who would take care of dinner?

If "who does what" is an issue in your relationship, I urge you to take some time alone together to create a system of delegation that works for both of you. In my book *If Love is a Game, These are the Rules*, I talked about creating win-win outcomes, which might be helpful for you to read about. Creating win-win outcomes means establishing a common goal and then finding creative solutions to make that goal happen. Since the shared goal here is the care of your children, much of what it comes down to is who is best suited for the task, or even who is available at the time the task needs to be done. For example, Betsy and Bob's son does karate every Tuesday night. It doesn't necessarily need to be one or the other who picks him up every Tuesday—it can be whoever gets out of work earlier. The same would hold true for making dinner. As for who patches the injuries . . . it probably depends on who is home when the kids come running in with a bloody nose, or a busted finger.

At the heart of negotiating responsibilities is the willingness of both partners to dedicate themselves to the bigger picture of a smoothly run family. That is the common goal, and everything else is just a means to that end. When both partners are willing to contribute, the "who does what" issue moves out of the realm of a problem and into the realm of a shared, cocreated life.

NEGOTIATING PARENTING STYLES

Many couples assume that because they love each other they share the same values, expectations, and beliefs about raising children. However, partners frequently have very different philosophies and ideas about parenting. After all, you probably got your ideas from watching your parents and thinking, "I will always . . ." or "I will never . . ." and you and your spouse may have had very different experiences growing up. What feels familiar and normal to you in terms of parenting may be alien to your spouse, and vice versa. Often couples are unaware of these discrepancies until they actually become parents themselves.

Everyone has different ways of doing things, and co-parenting can be challenging when your partner doesn't do things the way you do. For example, when Mary Beth and Jim had their first baby, Jim would go through four or five diapers before he got one on right. At first, Mary Beth would jump in and show him, "this is the way you do it," but she realized that she was undermining Jim's chance to learn to parent his own way. So she bit her lip and watched as Jim made it into a game each time, which made their baby laugh and laugh. By realizing that Mommy's way isn't the only way, Mary Beth gave Jim space to experience his own learning curve, and his confidence as a parent grew as a result.

Abby and Morgan experienced a clash in parenting styles on a deeper level. They were fairly similar in terms of temperament, likes, dislikes, and values, which is part of what attracted them to each other in the first place. They were both easygoing, tended toward alternative lifestyle choices, and placed a high valve on social consciousness. When they united their lives in marriage, it was a pretty smooth transition for both of them. When they were about to become parents, however, conflicts suddenly arose.

While they both agreed that they wanted to raise their daughter Chelsea consciously (aware and awake) and with kindness, Morgan's style was far more lenient than Abby's. He felt that whatever Chelsea did was okay, as long as she wasn't breaking the law. Abby, on the other hand, believed children needed to be taught limits, and things like making water balloons, throwing food, and hitting other children with her toys were not appropriate. Morgan accused Abby of being uptight, and she accused him of being careless in raising their child. They had never talked about their views on raising children, and when it came up they suddenly discovered these views were not in alignment.

It's always helpful to discuss your vision of parenting with your partner before you actually become parents. If you establish clear understandings and agreements before your child arrives, when life gets hectic, you will be ahead of the game.

I frequently ask couples who are about to become parents to align their differences and come to an agreement about their joint parenting styles. I've given many couples the following exercise, which you may also find helpful. Each partner needs to take time alone to answer the following questions. When you have given them sufficient thought and assessed your feelings, sit down together and discuss your individual responses. If you discover a lack of alignment, look for ways to negotiate so that each of you feels heard and has an equal share in the co-parenting arrangement.

Here are some key questions to address:

1. What are the happiest childhood memories that you want to re-create for our children?
2. What do you want to do differently from your own childhood?
3. What things did your parents do that you admired?
4. What values and morals do you want to transmit to our children?
5. How do you want to address religion with our children?
6. What approach to structure and discipline do you support?
7. How will you handle financial issues?
8. What roles do you specifically want to play in our children's lives, and what roles do you see me playing?
9. What legacy would you like to pass on to our children?

These questions will not address all parenting issues, but they do speak to many of the basic concerns that you may want to resolve before your child arrives. When you and your mate are aligned philosophically and practically, it makes decision-making easier and creates far less stress. Ideally, you can talk about this before you become parents, but if not, it's never too late to start this conversation.

Parents are not only the heads of the household, they are the captain and co-captain. If the parents at the helm of the ship are not aligned, then those under their care and guidance may become confused, uncertain, and fearful. When they present a united front, however, there is no limit to how far the family's ship can sail.

Having a child is a blessing that comes with dramatic changes. It will push you to clarify what you stand for and what you believe in, and test your ability to become a teammate with your partner. It will turn your world upside down, for certain, but it will also change your life for the better in more ways than you could ever imagine.

MOTHERHOOD IS
AN EXPERIENCE UNLIKE
ANY OTHER

Becoming a mother is a profound and unique adventure.

$\mathcal{M}$otherhood is an experience unlike any other on earth. There is nothing as profound, nothing that will stretch you so far beyond anything you previously imagined. It is remarkably challenging, yet uniquely rewarding at the same time. Other life experiences may bring you joy or fulfillment, or encourage you to grow, but none are on the same scale as becoming a mother.

When I began to write this book, a friend of mine in her early thirties who does not have children yet asked me how I would describe the experience of becoming a mother. It was a question that stopped me; after all, how could I describe the indescribable? How could I put into words what it is like to be the shepherd, the guardian, and the caretaker of a tiny, helpless human being . . . and to gradually wean and empower him or her to be able to live a healthy, happy, and successful life?

The answer is that there is no one definitive answer. In its most elevated state, motherhood is awesome. When you look up the definition of "awesome," the dictionary says: "so impressive or overwhelming as to inspire a strong feeling of admiration or fear; grand, moving, frightening, majestic and lofty." This is the most inspirational element of motherhood—the soul-stirring aura of greatness that makes it so hard to define.

Yet the job of mother most often plays itself out not on the lofty levels of Hallmark splendor, but rather in the trenches of day-to-day life. The greatest adventure lies somewhere between the peanut butter and jelly sandwiches and the teaching of life lessons. Some days will be a placid and lazy cruise down the river, others will be a wild and furious ride through the rapids. One day you'll think you have it all figured out, and that, of course, is the day your son comes home with a note from his teacher alerting you to the fact that he is failing four subjects. Just when you think you can't take it anymore, a hand-made Mother's Day card appears like a rainbow in a stormy sky. And right at the point when it all seems to come together, you take a second look and realize your baby is all grown up and in need of your services in an entirely different way.

I can compare motherhood to any number of things: a diamond with many facets, an adventure, a miracle, a graduate course in the school of life. The truth is that it is all of these things and more. The process is unique to each woman, and no two mothers have the same exact experience. It is a rite of passage, a whole new level of responsibility, and a chance to explore and exercise your personal choices. However you experience the role of mother, you can be certain that it will be quite different from any other you have played in your life up until now.

A New Level of Responsibility

Making a decision to have a child—it's momentous. It is to decide forever to have your heart walking around outside your body. ELIZABETH STONE

I remember when my neighbor Ivy got a puppy a few years ago. She'd always wanted one, and when she and her boyfriend of four years split up, it seemed the right time to get herself a loving canine companion. She imagined how the dog would curl up at her feet an night, greet her with joy when she came home, and fill the "cuddle void" in her life. So she went to the local pound and got a Labrador retriever puppy she named Skipper.

Three weeks after Ivy brought Skipper home, I saw her walking him around the block and I stopped to say hello. Ivy looked exhausted! I asked her how the training was going, and she told me she was amazed at how much work went into training a puppy. She was shocked when she realized that she couldn't take her eyes off him for one second. He was curious and wanted to chew everything in sight, and it was her responsibility to teach him what was and was not allowed. We laughed together when I told her she was getting her first glimpse at motherhood.

Having a child is different from buying a plant, getting a dog, or even getting married. A plant requires only the time it takes to water it. A puppy needs the survival basics of food, water, walking, petting, bathing, and visits to the vet. Having a husband or partner comes the closest, in that it requires the advanced skills of communication, negotiation, give and take, nurturing, love, and intimacy. From love relationships, we learn how to incorporate an "other" into our innermost frame of reference. Becoming a mother is different, however, in that it requires all of you.

Motherhood is a unique relationship that involves total commitment. It is a twenty-four-hour-a-day, seven-day-a-week job that begins the moment your child is born and doesn't end until the day you leave this world. It doesn't cease when you go to sleep. You don't really get breaks, unless you have child care or help from a family member. The responsibility doesn't stop when your child has her own home or her own family. Wherever you are, whatever you do, a small part of you is always aware that there is another being on this planet who is under your care and whose well-being affects you as much as your own does.

Though my daughter Jennifer is grown and on her own at college across the country, I am always aware of her. I can be on the road giving workshops, lecturing or facilitating a group, at home writing on my computer or having fun with my husband and friends, but she is always in my consciousness. Sometimes she is right in the center of my awareness, like when I know she is in the middle of a big challenge or right after we hang up the phone. Other times she skirts around the edges of my mind and heart. No matter how far apart we are or how independent she is, she will always be my daughter.

The intense connection between a mother and her children brings with it a new level of responsibility. You are the one who watches over them, teaches them, and guides them. You are the person who nurtures their spiritual core and their well-being. You are responsible not only for making sure they know right from wrong and have a good sense of self-esteem, but also for seeing that they are wearing warm enough clothes and that they drink their milk. In the beginning, even their basic survival is your responsibility.

For many new mothers, responsibility shows up first in caretaking. During the first few months of your baby's life, you learn how to meet his basic survival needs, which includes how to feed him, bathe him, care for him when he is ill, and soothe him into sleep at night. There is so much at first that goes into ensuring that this tiny being is safe and healthy. Like any other new skill set, it takes time to learn, and it can be overwhelming.

Tracy, a 25-year-old mother of a newborn, found the new level of responsibility scary. When she was pregnant, she didn't really think clearly about how things would be after the birth. She knew she would need to learn to care for her baby, but she never really absorbed the fact that his very survival depended upon her. When she and her husband, Peter, first brought their baby, Jack, home, like so many other couples they were overwhelmed. Jack's basic needs were simple, but when you added them all up, there was a lot to do. Between creating a feeding schedule, changing diapers, ensuring good sleep patterns, bathing, stimulation, fresh air, doctor visits, and everything else that must get done in an average day, life seemed like a roller coaster of new responsibilities. As time passed, the caretaking started to become more natural, but Tracy clearly remembers that it took a real shift in her thinking for her to be able to step into this new level of responsibility.

"I can absolutely remember one day suddenly thinking, 'Wow, this is another human being who is entirely dependent on me,' " she recalls. "It was a real shocker to think that Peter and I were the ones who were totally in charge of Jack's life, health, and safety."

The good news is that the first few months pass rather quickly. As that first learning curve comes to an end, however, new challenges, tasks, and responsibilities arise. Next comes the duty of keeping your child safe, both within your home and outside in the world. Then comes the challenge of teaching her—to walk, to hold utensils, to drink from a cup, to use a toilet, to talk. And so it goes from there, indefinitely. The specifics change with age and time, but the overall responsibility is there, in varying ways, until they are grown and able to care for themselves and beyond.

As a mother, you never really stop feeling responsible for your children. I know a woman with a 52-year-old son who still worries because he doesn't wear a hat when it snows. No matter how old our children get, in some ways they are always our babies. We see very clearly how they have matured and grown and created lives of their own, but the mother in us always holds them and their care in our consciousness.

A Rite of Passage

I love being a mother . . . I am more aware. I feel things on a deeper level. I have a kind of understanding about my body, about being a woman.

SHELLEY LONG

Motherhood initiates you into a very exclusive club. It gives you an entreé into a sisterhood of women who understand to some degree what you are experiencing, who know in their hearts and souls at least something of what you are feeling, thinking, and hoping. Motherhood connects you to the most primal and spiritual part of your humanness and advances your life lessons tenfold.

Becoming a mother involves a passing of the torch. Up until now, you have played the role of daughter in the mother/daughter equation. Now it is finally your turn to mother someone else, and that transition is one of the major ones in your life. You move from the dependent, receiving end of the continuum to the giving, guiding end. You become an autonomous giver, teacher, and authority figure. You reach another level of adulthood in that you become the parent of another, and create a new link in the chain of life.

When you become a mother, it may call to light your relationship with your own mother. As you step into a new version of the role she played in your life (or didn't play, depending on your circumstances), you may find yourself thinking about that relationship in new ways. It may cause you to identify with her as you never have before. For Helena, a 29-year-old teacher, the birth of her twin girls gave her a whole new appreciation of how much work it must have been for her mother to raise her and her three siblings. She became acutely aware of the endless details involved, and was amazed to think about her mother managing four children all under the age of five at the same time. Her parents had had a very traditional marriage, in which her father went to work every day and her mother stayed home and raised the children by herself. She had always secretly judged her mother for being a "housewife" and not having a job outside the home. Yet now that she and her husband were juggling two newborns together, she realized that her mother had managed a job just as demanding as Helena's by herself and she respected her for it.

When Jackie became a mother, she finally understood what her own mother had meant all those years when she said things like "you'll never know how much I worry," and "if I could take the pain from you and keep it myself, I would." She'd always dismissed those as what she called "Momisms"—sayings that all mothers are programmed to deliver. But when her five-year-old broke his arm while playing hockey, she actually found herself wishing she could have taken his pain from him rather than his having to endure the torture of having it set in the emergency room.

The link between mothers and daughters is a powerful one. After all, it is your own mother who taught you by example how to be a mother. Hopefully, you learned things from her that were positive—things that you would like to emulate, as in Renée's or Beverly's case. Renée's mother was very creative and always came up with innovative ways to teach Renée and her brothers. Renée remembers her mother teaching her the alphabet by assembling 26 items, each one beginning with a different letter of the alphabet, on the kitchen table and making it a game for her to put the items in alphabetical order. Renée knows she wants to use as many of her mother's creative parenting methods as she can remember.

Beverly credits her mother with instilling in her a strong sense of self. Her mother made efforts to continually validate Beverly's ideas and opinions. She remembers her mother giving her choices early in life, which taught her to discover her own likes and dislikes and encouraged her to find her own voice. For example, one night each week, Beverly chose the family dinner menu. Though the other six nights she would have to eat whatever was prepared, on "her" night, she got to choose—even if that meant her parents ate spaghetti or bologna sandwiches. Now Beverly makes sure she gives her children the opportunity to choose whenever possible so that they can develop their decision-making abilities.

WORKING THROUGH
MOTHER/DAUGHTER ISSUES

Transitioning from daughter to mother can be a little tricky, especially if you haven't really addressed your "mother issues." In order to prepare yourself for motherhood, it helps to first take a close look at your past relationship with your mother. All of us—even those with the most wonderful mothers in the world—need to examine this relationship if we are to effectively mother our own children. The mothering template you have is a legacy passed along by your own mother, consciously or unconsciously. Once you are aware of it, it's up to you to preserve that legacy or revise it. Ideally, we want to pass along the lessons and values that we most appreciated from our mothers, and revise the patterns of behavior that were not ideal.

Nancy and her 15-year-old daughter, Cassie, came to see me to work through some of the tension they were experiencing in their relationship. Though much of their conflict was normal for parents and typical teenagers, one issue that arose again and again was driving a serious wedge between them. Hardly a day went by without screaming arguments and tears, and Nancy was out of ideas. So she brought a very reluctant Cassie with her to meet with me, to see if we could get to the heart of what was going on and create some solutions.

The minute they sat down in front of me, Cassie's anger was apparent. She sat with her arms crossed and refused to look directly at her mother. When Nancy started to tell me about how uncomfortable things had become between them, I gently stopped her and asked Cassie to tell me her side of the story. At first she seemed a little surprised that I'd asked for her input, but then she proceeded to describe her reality:

"Nothing I ever do is right as far as she's concerned," she said, motioning with her head toward her mother. "She just rips on me all day long. She hates my hair. She hates my clothes—says I dress like a homeless person. Last week, right in front of my friends, she says your face is all broken out again—like I don't know that! Everywhere we go she yells at me to pick my feet up when I walk or to stand up straight, and I'm so sick of it."

Cassie went on for a while, telling me about how Nancy never left her alone, and when she seemed spent, I turned to Nancy.

"Is what Cassie just described an accurate description in your eyes?" I asked.

"Of course not!" Nancy replied. "She makes it sound like I'm the Wicked Witch of the West. All I'm trying to do is teach her good grooming habits, so people have a good impression of her. I want her to be the best she can be, and so I make suggestions. Is that so terrible?"

"No," Cassie interrupted. "But think about how upset you get every time Grandma takes a jab at you!"

In her 15-year-old wisdom, Cassie laid out in front of Nancy the pattern that she was repeating from her own experience growing up. Nancy's mother grew up during the Depression and had developed a hardened approach to life. She was an eternal pessimist who rarely dispensed compliments. She was stern and demanding toward Nancy and her sister and rarely tolerated anything less than perfect behavior. To this day, when Nancy calls her mother with good news about her job or her children, her mother always has some sort of negative response.

Without realizing it, Nancy had internalized her mother's way of relating to her children. In her conscious mind, Nancy believed she was just trying to help Cassie, but beneath the surface, old family dynamics were at play. She was applying the same rigid and impossible standards to her daughter that her mother had applied to her.

Once she excavated this pattern, Nancy was free to choose how she would proceed. She could choose to continue the dynamic that had developed between Cassie and her, or she could take steps to communicate differently. The shift could not happen, however, until Nancy was willing to look at her relationship with her own mother to see where she might have picked up any negative imprinting.

The collective unconscious from your family culture can be handed down right along with the china and linens without your ever being fully aware of it. When you sort through and become aware of the hidden expectations and dynamics you bring to the table, you can assess what is missing and take deliberate steps to supply what is needed.

You can start with the following questions:

1. What did you appreciate about your mother?
2. What do you wish had been different?
3. What do you think was your mother's philosophy or approach to raising you?
4. What are the things your mother did that you want to emulate?
5. What would you like to do differently?
6. What qualities would you include on your "ideal mothering" list?

Excavating these answers allows you to choose the legacies you want to pass along and those you want to change. You can discover where you identify with your own mother, and where you want to break links of behavior that might have been passed on. You can take what you loved about her and her mothering and consciously go forward to create your own vision that incorporates these elements.

Alex was 23 and expecting her first child when she took my Inner Negotiation Workshop. She was looking ahead to her impending role as a mother, and she took the workshop so she could become clear about what kind of mother she wanted to be. Alex completed her lists in response to the questions above, and I would like to share them with you as an example. Your lists will no doubt be different from hers; I am offering these merely to stimulate your own thoughts on the subject.

Alex's lists:

What I appreciated about my mother:

1. The way she took care of me when I was sick. She used to bring a snack tray into my room with soup and crackers, and snuggle with me and watch game shows on television until I got better.
2. The stories she would make up at bedtime with all the people and animals that I knew.
3. She always read to me and taught me to love books.
4. Her blueberry cobbler.
5. Her sense of adventure. She made everything fun.
6. The fact that she found the time to be a leader of my Brownie troop.

What I wish had been different:

1. I wish she had played more kid stuff with me like going to the zoo or just playing games.
2. I wish she had helped me with my homework. She always left that to Dad, but she was a really good teacher and had a way of making things make sense.
3. I wish she had talked to me more about the important things in life, about men, sex, and how to be a woman.
4. I wish she had explained why she said "no" to certain things, instead of just making hers the last word.
5. I wish she had encouraged me to be more assertive.

The things my mother did that I want to emulate:

1. I want to have her style and grace.
2. I want to always have flowers around me the way she did.
3. I want to always show my love for my children regardless of what they do.
4. I want to bake with my child, and teach him or her to do other creative things.
5. I want to read to and with my child.
6. I want to be adventurous and make life fun for my child.

The things I would like to do differently:

1. I would like to take time out to talk to my child about what to expect in life, and to prepare him or her for what lies ahead.

2. I want to listen more to what my child is saying, both with words and in actions.
3. I want to encourage my children to be independent and to stand up for themselves.
4. I want my children feel they have a say in their own lives, that I am not a dictator.
5. I do not plan to use physical punishment.
6. I do not want to judge my children as good or bad; I want to accept them exactly the way they are, regardless of whether it is in alignment with what I would hope for.

The type of mother I want to be:

1. I want to be fun, playful, supportive, loving, and kind.
2. I want to be generous without going overboard, strong without being overpowering, gentle without being weak, compassionate without being a pushover.
3. I want to be a role model—to live the way I want to inspire them to live.
4. I want to create an environment where we all learn from everything that happens to us.
5. I want to be smart about financial matters and teach my children to be also.
6. I want to be approachable and willing to negotiate.
7. I want my children to know they can tell me anything without fear of being judged.
8. I want to encourage their growth, and be their emotional guide.

Based on how your mother raised you, there may be plenty of wonderful traits you want to emulate, or there may be many that you want to change. The beauty of becoming clear on what you were unconsciously taught is that you can keep all the best traits of the woman who raised you and improve upon them. Imagine how much better our parenting skills will be in generations to come if we all take the time to make conscious choices like these now! It's up to you: do you choose to continue as a link in your family's behavioral chain, or is it time for a change?

LIVING YOUR VISION

After you have created a vision of your own ideal version of "Mom," then it is time to put your vision into action. This is the hard part. What looks easy on paper can be a challenge to implement in real life, and this is where the real work begins.

It's one thing to say what kind of mother you want to be; it's something entirely different to actually put that plan into action on a daily basis. Motherhood is practiced daily, not unlike any other spiritual discipline. There will be days when you feel aligned with your vision of who you want to be as a mother, and others when you might feel like you are failing miserably. What matters most is that you show up every day and try again.

Strategy is important when it comes to implementing any vision. The first step is always to weed out anything that might be standing in your way. When you know where you want to go, you can see what obstacles might be in your way. For instance, if part of your vision of being a mother includes spending weekends with your child and your schedule is preventing you from doing so, you'll need to look at what adjustments you can make in order to realize your original vision. You may need to take a step back and assess how you allocate your time so that you can notice where you may be shortchanging your children and yourself. Perhaps you can scale back some other activities, or get approval to work at home one day a week.

Grace's vision of motherhood included being a good listener. It was important to her that her children feel she was always there for them—a person to turn to for advice or a loving and nonjudgmental ear. Yet that rarely happened. Instead, the scenario went something like this: one of her four children would start to talk to her, and suddenly another one would appear with a question or a need, to say "hello" or get some of the attention. The link between Grace and the child in need would be temporarily interrupted, and more often than not the conversation was terminated or simply faded away.

The situation was frustrating to Grace, so she examined what was standing in the way of her living her vision. She realized a lack of boundaries between the children was the problem, so she set up what she called "private time" with each child. If they needed her, all they needed to do was ask for "private time," and they would get an uninterrupted audience with Mom. Grace and the child would go into his or her bedroom, hang a "private time" sign that Grace made with magic markers and a piece of cardboard, and be able to talk without being distracted. Grace's family loved this idea so much that they made two separate signs—"Mom private time" and "Dad private time"—to get Grace's husband in on the plan.

How can you stay aligned with your vision, even in the midst of the chaos of daily life? Perhaps you can create a physical representation of your vision, like a written "mission statement" or a "vision map," and post it somewhere you can see it. A woman in my workshop created a vision map that included the elements of motherhood she aspired to and hung it on the bulletin board in her home office. She chose a magazine picture of a woman walking through the woods with her child to remind her that she wanted to share her love of nature. Then she found a photo of her husband with their daughter picking out a pumpkin for Halloween to remind her that holidays are for families regardless of deadlines or social engagements. She included various quotations that have special meaning for her. Every time she looks up at that collage, she realigns with her vision of motherhood.

You may also want to consider keeping a journal to document the times you deviate from your vision of how you want to be. Keeping a journal enables you to reflect on your behavior and provides you with a dose of reality. When you see your innermost thoughts and feelings, as well as recollections of past events, you can achieve a certain level of objectivity. Use your journal as a tool for self-discovery. It's your receptacle for the conversations in your mind, and a place you can go for a reality check. It can be your psychological and emotional "mirror." You can use it to record accomplishments that make you proud, and to see when and where you are veering off course from your vision of how you ideally want to mother your child.

Lastly, when it is appropriate, let your child be your guide. She will be the first to let you know how you are doing! Lori was standing out on the sidewalk with a friend of hers and both of their three-year-old girls. They had just come out of ballet practice and discovered it was raining, which made it nearly impossible to find a taxi. All four of them were getting drenched, when suddenly Lori spotted an available taxi down the street. She ran down the street and hailed the taxi. As her friend shepherded the two little girls in beside her, Lori realized with horror that she had just bolted without a word and left her daughter standing there in the rain. Granted, she was with her friend, but Lori was mortified that she had run down the street on impulse without telling her daughter that she would be right back.

"Oh, my god . . . I'm the world's worst mommy!" she wailed to her friend.

Lori's little girl heard this and opened her big brown eyes as wide as they would go.

She threw her arms around Lori's neck, and said, "No you're not! You're the best mommy! We're dry now 'cause you got us a taxi. You're the best mommy in the whole world!"

Listen to your children—if they tell you you're doing just fine, believe them. After all, it's their opinion that really counts.

Making Your Own Choices

Most mothers are instinctive philosophers.   HARRIET BEECHER STOWE

The final element that separates motherhood from all the other experiences in life is this: with nothing else will other people feel so free to tell you their opinions on what you should and should not do!

When it comes to raising children, everyone has an opinion. All parents have their systems, their little tricks and methods, their philosophies and beliefs. And they all believe that their way is best. You can be certain that the moment you become a mother, there will be plenty of people not only willing to give you advice, but who will come right out and tell you exactly how you should proceed in raising your child.

Paige's son, Will, was born with a facial deformity that the doctor said could be fixed when Will was two years old. Shortly after Will's second birthday, Paige and her husband decided to have the surgery done. There were only slight risks involved, and they wanted him to have as normal a life as possible. When their friends and family found out, everyone suddenly felt free to offer up their opinion. Paige's mother said she was crazy to risk surgery, that Will would adjust. Her mother-in-law said he should definitely have the surgery, but not until he was a little older. Her friend told her she'd heard about another doctor in a nearby city who had performed the surgery using a better technique. The unsolicited advice went on and on, and Paige started to doubt her decision. Were they doing the right thing? Should they wait? Should they go to this other doctor? Eventually they went forward with the surgery, but only after Paige told everyone politely but firmly to keep their opinions to themselves.

Motherhood is one of life's best opportunities to hone your ability to make your own choices. After you've read the books and talked to your pediatrician, your mother, your friends, and the nice lady next door who raised a family of ten, it comes down to this: how do you want to raise your children?

Motherhood is a rite of passage that offers us a chance to examine the past and choose our own future. As we look back at the mothering we ourselves received or lacked, we can begin to make conscious choices about how we want to relate to our own children, and how we want to handle the new level of responsibility bestowed upon us.

There are so many elements that set motherhood apart from all the other passages in your life. Though you may have had practice in your love relationships, it's not quite the same for, as a mother, you are ultimately responsible for this little human being. All that you know, believe, and feel goes into your mothering, yet it is ultimately unlike anything you have experienced before. It is truly a profound and unique adventure.

A MOTHER HAS MANY ROLES

Raising a child is a multifaceted job.

WANTED: Patient, dedicated woman to donate her body for the development, nurturing, guidance, and care of a new person. Must be capable of extreme multitasking. Duties include loving, supporting, encouraging self-esteem, mentoring, guidance counseling, and tutoring. Domestic skills required include but are not limited to: cleaning, cooking, laundry, ironing, sewing, nursing, chauffeuring (or the ability to manage someone else doing all of these tasks). Expectations must include sharing joys and disappointments, celebrating all firsts and rites of passage, imparting wisdom at appropriate moments, and disciplining when appropriate. Applicant must be tender, tough, wise, playful, eager to teach and learn, comforting, compassionate, worthy of respect, unafraid of getting hands dirty, and above all, flexible. Perfectionists need not apply.

*D*oes this sound like a job you might like to apply for? Well, congratulations! As a mother, you're already hired!

Whether you run a Fortune 500 company, mastermind the greatest website in the cyberuniverse, or minister to the dying in developing countries, being a mother is still the most challenging job you will ever have. It is tough work, demands huge amounts of your time, attention, energy, and patience, and is rarely what you anticipated. The good news, however, is that it also yields the greatest joys imaginable.

As a mother, you will play many roles. The following is a short list of some of the ones you will most likely fulfill in the course of your child's life:

Caretaker

Nurse

Chauffeur

Protector

Teacher

Short-order cook

Wardrobe consultant

Disciplinarian

Tutor

Videographer

Cheerleader

Social secretary

Seamstress/costume designer

Life organizer

Referee

Confidant
Life guide
Mentor
Friend

Many women must add the role of "income earner" or "financial supporter" to the list, which of course makes the job that much more complicated.

Ultimately, a mother's purpose is to assure that her baby becomes a fully functional, mature adult. This includes ensuring that this little person is healthy, happy, clean, loved, safe, secure, provided for, nourished, stimulated, nurtured, well cared for, exposed to opportunities, and able to grow in a positive, healthy, and productive manner. All the roles you play are the means to this specific goal.

Raising a child requires many skills and will at times demand everything you have to give. Thankfully, though, you probably won't have to use all your skills simultaneously (unless you have triplets, and that's a whole other story). One day will require tolerance while the next calls for sharing a triumph. One day is about creating fun, and the next is about negotiating chores. At times you will be the shoulder they cry on and other moments you will be the person who sets limits or reprimands. One year might require endless hours of caretaking when your child suffers from an extended illness, while another year might be all about showing up for important life passages. It's really all about being flexible and paying attention to what is required from you at the time.

Throughout the time that my daughter Jennifer was growing up,

I was a single mother; hence, all the joys and responsibilities fell squarely on my shoulders. I was the one who was there when she took her first step, said her first word, and skied down her first slope. I was the one who came into her room in the middle of the night and saw her in a sea of vomit; I spent the rest of the night cleaning her, the bedding, and the room, holding and reassuring her. I was the one who drove frantically to the doctor's office when she spilled a scalding cup of water on herself. I was the one who was there when her braces came off, the one who took her to the emergency room when she complained of stomach cramps. I begged the doctor to see her when she was screaming at the top of her lungs, only to find out that she was passing a kidney stone at the tender age of 13! I was the one she told about her first kiss. I was the one who drove her to jazz class, club volleyball at 5 A.M. Saturday morning, to and from schools from the age of five on. I was the one who watched her learn to swim under water like a little fish and the one who organized annual, memorable birthday parties so she would feel treasured. I was the one who listened when she wasn't picked for the team, and felt as if I'd failed myself. I taught her how to drive a stick shift and astound everyone with her driving ability. I was the one who said "no" to a coed sleepover when she was 13. I helped her create her costume as Eleanor Roosevelt in her class play, and then years later cheered her for writing her paper on Hillary Clinton. I took her trick-or-treating in different costumes every year, and I was Santa, the Easter Bunny, and the tooth fairy. Throughout it all, I needed to fulfill all these roles, and more.

That's only a small fraction of the roles I played, and I'm sure, as a mother, your own list will be just as long. Very few life experiences teach you to be "everything" to someone quite like motherhood does.

The Roles a Mother Plays

God could not be everywhere and therefore he made mothers.

JEWISH PROVERB

Knowing which role is required at what time will depend entirely on the situation at hand. I can't tell you what role to play any more than I can predict the fluctuations of the stock market. It's an instinct that you develop as time goes by. Eventually, what is required comes to you at the right moment as naturally as breathing. The secret is paying attention to what your child needs at the moment and being flexible enough to respond accordingly.

Susan became frustrated with her eight-year-old, Ryan, after he spilled soda on the living room couch. Ryan knew he wasn't allowed to bring food or drinks into the living room, and that the accident could be costly. She reprimanded Ryan, letting him know in no uncertain terms that she was not happy with his behavior, then sent him outside so she could begin cleaning the mess.

Susan was still annoyed twenty minutes later (the stain wasn't coming out no matter how hard she scrubbed) when Ryan ran back into the house and straight up to his room. Concerned, Susan followed Ryan upstairs and found him sobbing on his bed. Through the sobs and gasps, Ryan told her he'd gotten booted off the neighborhood T-ball team because he missed one critical catch. Her son was clearly miserable, and it took a fraction of a second for Susan to switch from her role of disciplinarian to her role of "source of comfort and compassion." Earlier, Ryan needed boundaries; now he needed to be comforted. Susan didn't need to consciously decide to switch gears; it happened automatically. She scooped Ryan up in her arms, held him, and patted his back while he cried about his plight.

Let's take a look at some of the more prominent roles you'll play as a mother.

CARETAKER

You are the primary source of care for your child. You are responsible for ensuring that your child is fed, clothed, safe, and healthy. You are the person who is there when everyone else has only reasons and excuses. You can delegate responsibility for nourishment, stimulation, cleaning, dressing, and baby-sitting, but ultimately you are the one who is responsible for your child's *life*.

Of course, the father is also responsible for the care of your child, and many husbands do act as partners in raising children. What I am referring to here, however, is the role of *primary* caretaker: the one who ultimately runs the show. There are scenarios where the father is the primary caretaker, where he stays home and cares for the children and the mother goes to work, or where a single father raises the children. However, most often in our society, it is the mother who fulfills this role. This may be so for any number of reasons, ranging from sexual politics to biology to social structures. What is so interesting is the fact that so many women actively choose to take on this role. Years ago it may have been thrust upon them with no say, but today it seems to be more about choice and less about stereotypical mandates.

The role of caretaker includes all physical aspects of your child's existence. Sometimes you will intuit what is needed, other times you will hear it loud and clear, and still other times you will be clueless about what to do for your little one. Responding in a timely manner means that you respect your child's needs, attend to them, and let him know that someone deeply cares about his well-being and happiness.

Throughout the preverbal months, the only way children can communicate is with their lungs and their cries for help. When Jennifer was eight months old, we visited my sister in Colorado. One evening, Jennifer started to cry. We had no idea what was wrong. We changed her diapers, gave her a bottle, sang to her, tried to rock her to sleep, took her outside for a walk, and nothing worked. After about an hour and a half, I looked at her and said, "Please send me a message in my head so I can know what to do for you." Moments later, I had a flash of insight that said, "change her clothes." She was wearing yellow pajamas with feet. I changed her into a pink nightgown that was open at the bottom, and she instantly stopped crying. I still am not sure if it was the feet of the PJs, the texture of the fabric, or the color pink, but changing her pajamas worked.

Listening to what they are trying to communicate, hearing what is not said, feeling their frustration, letting them know that you are there, that you love them through it all, and that you are not going away—these are the things that matter most. I was recently on a plane when I observed a mother with a six-month-old child. The child was squirming, and the mother was wrestling with her trying to get her to sit still. The more the mother restrained the child, the more the child squirmed, squealed, and resisted. It was becoming a real battle. I traveled extensively with Jennifer from the time she was a baby, so over the years I had learned a few things about babies on planes. I leaned across the aisle and said, "Can I help?"

She looked at me, exasperated, and said, "I just don't know what to do. I've tried everything."

I said, "If she will come to me, I think I may be able to help." She handed me her baby, knowing that we were both trapped on the same plane and figuring I had at least a 50–50 chance of success. I asked the child's name and was told it was Jeannie. I started to talk to Jeannie in a soothing voice; then I stood up and walked with her, pointing out things on the plane. I pointed to the luggage compartment, the design in the rug, the tray tables, the video screen, the food and beverages. Then I pointed to the flight attendants and the other passengers. I never stopped talking to her, and as I held her gently yet firmly, I redirected her attention to things other than herself. Within a few minutes she quieted down and started to look at those people and things that I was pointing to. This is a technique I learned with Jennifer, who required constant stimulation and no restraints. I became her in-flight tour guide, who gave her attention yet focused her on people, places, and things that took her attention off her own discomfort.

The root of the caretaker role is "care." To care means to give comfort, assistance, affection, and attention to another. The secret to learning to be an effective caretaker for your child is to tap into your inner wisdom and give this little being whatever you sense she needs to feel safe and secure, and to know she is loved.

LIFE GUIDE

They're watching. They watch everything you say and do. Whether you're aware of it or not, they watch your every move, gesture, breath, word, tone of voice, frown, and smile. They're watching when you don't notice, when you can't imagine, when you least suspect; they're watching, listening, and recording everything about you. It's no wonder that "the apple doesn't fall far from the tree"!

Your imprint on them is stronger than that of any other person in the world. They watch you pack for a trip, make your to-do list, balance your checkbook, or sit and read a book. They watch you bite your nails, yell at random drivers on the freeway, or watch TV eating ice cream. They listen to your grammar, your word choice, and your tone. They watch what you do, and how you do it, and they imitate your mannerisms. They absorb whatever you do and incorporate it into their consciousness as the norm.

They look at the world through a filter that is created by you. You lead by your example. You transmit your values by the words you say along with the actions you take. As their role model, it is up to you to instill values in them.

Being the primary role model for another human being is an

enormous task. It means that you not only have to tell them what to do and what not to do, you also have to pay attention to what *you* do. Children are smart: if you dictate one way of behaving and display another, they'll catch on, and will most likely follow your actions rather than your words.

Mindy had always told her children not to swear. She had a six-year-old son who understood that "cursing wasn't nice," and a two-year-old daughter who was just beginning to speak in phrases. One day, Mindy was driving with her daughter in the car and another driver cut her off and stole the parking space she was about to pull into. She banged the wheel with her hand and said, "Oh, sh__!" Mindy assumed her daughter was too young to understand what she had said.

A few days later, Mindy was in the kitchen feeding her daughter. The bowl accidentally fell from the table and landed on the floor. To her shock, Mindy's daughter banged her hand on the tray of her high chair and said, "Oh, sh__!" Mindy laughed—she couldn't help it. The sight of this little one voicing such an expletive was pretty funny, but Mindy realized she'd need to be more careful about what she said around her. Never doubt it, they're always watching and listening.

Ask yourself what you want to telegraph to your children. What values do you want to send them? What messages do you want them to absorb? The more clarity you have about this, the more you will be able to be conscious about what you transmit to them. By turning the mirror inward, you can see what it is that you are projecting outward to your child.

If you are married or have a parenting partner, it's helpful to develop a set of "house rules" together. For instance, your list might look something like this:

1. Swear words are not used in our home (specify which words).
2. Drugs are unacceptable.
3. Alcohol is to be used in moderation (stipulate amounts).
4. People will be addressed in a respectful tone.
5. Animals should be treated with kindness.
6. Dishonesty is not tolerated.

You'll need to do your part and actually live by these rules yourself. Your children will always follow what you do more easily than they will follow what you say. If you don't adhere to the principles you are preaching, chances are, neither will they.

For children's first five or so years, the most significant imprints come from family. Your home is their universe, and it is there that they learn values and behaviors that will be the foundation for the rest of their lives. When television becomes a factor they will copy words, expressions, and attitudes from the shows they watch. After children start school, peers and teachers become strong influences. When they start going to friends' homes, to movies, to the mall, their world becomes enlarged again, and they start to absorb the attitudes, behaviors, opinions, and beliefs of this larger circle. If you see them rescuing a hurt animal, ask yourself where they learned this. If you see them acting out in hostile or violent ways, ask yourself where those behaviors were observed and reinforced—and possibly even rewarded. It is up to you to see what and who is influencing and impacting them.

In *Reviving Ophelia*, Mary Pipher, Ph.D., suggests that the messages the media presents to young people are antithetical to the messages parents are trying to instill. Realizing how impressionable your child is, along with the fact that you can't be there twenty-four hours a day, makes it all the more urgent to establish values at an early age. There are some children who can differentiate between what they see in the media and actual daily life, and there are others who can't. When your child is exposed to violence, it is a good idea to monitor his response. Talk to him and find out if he can make the distinction between what he sees and the decisions he will make. Many children see action heroes solve all their problems with guns and violence; they connect with this and imitate the hero's behaviors. If you observe alarming behaviors, don't brush them aside: seek professional help immediately in the early stages in order to turn these behaviors around before it's too late.

Your child looks to you to show him how to travel down the road of life. You will have his complete attention and total absorption until he approaches his teens. The actress Jill Eikenberry once said, "You have a wonderful child. Then, when he's 13, gremlins carry him away and leave in his place a stranger who gives you not a moment's peace." Around the teen years, your child will begin to resist your guidance, even fight your every request. Whether following your lead and taking cues from you or resisting your guidance, he is trying to figure out who he is, and what he thinks, believes, and feels.

You are the one who shows the way with your attitudes, behaviors, responses to situations, and the alignment of your words with your actions. The teen years are when children truly need your life guidance, although that is the time when they resist it the most.

TEACHER

Whether you think of yourself as a teacher or not, you are. A big part of your job as mother is to teach, train, and coach. Whether you teach your child how to tie her shoes, ride a bike, or know the difference between right and wrong, whether you potty train your child, teach her to say "no" to drugs, or to drive a car, you are providing the handrails that she will grasp onto for the rest of her life.

You, as a mother, are the primary person who shapes your child's behavior. Motivating your child, reinforcing desirable behaviors, discouraging negative or destructive ones, are all part of what a mother does. You are not the only one who does this, but you are the *essential* and overarching entity whose imprint goes the deepest within the psyche of your child.

Teaching involves imparting information. But more than the transfer of knowledge, it requires empowering a person to use the information they receive. When teaching children, you want to observe their optimum learning mode. Some children learn kinesthetically, or with hands-on manipulation of 3-D objects. Others learn visually, while still others learn auditorily. Regardless of your learning style, pay attention to the manner in which your child absorbs information. If you want to maximize the results, you will gear your teaching toward your child's style, rather than your own.

Lois was Terri's mother. Lois was a visual learner. She learned by reading books and looking at diagrams. Lois hated having people read to her. She was happiest when given a manual and allowed to learn on her own. Terri was the type of person who learned by doing. If she could have contact with an object and have a personal coach walk her through the steps, she was happy. So when Terri was 12 she asked her mother to help her learn to use a computer program that made greeting cards. Her mother gave her the manual and said, "There you go." Terri couldn't understand what she was supposed to do with the manual, so it sat on her bookshelf. When I met with both Lois and Terri, I found it interesting to observe the disconnection between the two. Lois said, "I gave her the manual, but she never even looked at it." Terri said, "I asked her for help, and all she did was give me some dumb manual." Obviously what worked for Lois didn't work for Terri, and vice versa.

Children from birth to the age of six are totally open to learning everything you and their environment have to teach. They have no filters and are wide open to all information. The more exposure and stimulation caretakers can provide for them, the happier they are. When children are left alone without a guide to stimulate their mental processes, they are not challenged and therefore become cranky and learn to seek attention in negative ways. The more opportunities you can provide for them that involve observation, interaction, stimulation, and positive recognition the more interested and interesting they become.

Learning opportunities abound every day; however, you must recognize them. A learning opportunity is seeing a door open in your child's mind when it is ready to absorb a morsel of life's wisdom. If you take a few moments, you can position something that you dearly want your child to know. It usually starts by your child asking a question. You have the choice of how to respond. You can defer learning opportunities until later, telling him something to pacify him, or you can stop what you are doing, connect, and give him the information he is seeking. These moments are fleeting, and as quick as the doors to learning open, they close just as quickly. If you see the moments, seize them and respond appropriately—you will get immediate results from giving your children a full 100 percent of your attention.

Martha and her son Anthony were spending the afternoon together running errands. As they were leaving the dry cleaner, they got in the car and he turned to her and said, "Why can't I have a computer like Tyler?" She realized that right next door to the dry cleaner was a computer store. This was a moment that she could either brush off or use as a learning opportunity. "The reason we haven't bought a computer is because there are many things to discuss beforehand. We have to see which brand is the right one for us, find out how much they cost, set aside the money, see where the computer will go, and learn how to use it. You see, Anthony, a computer is a big investment. Before buying it, we want to make sure that we are fully informed. Would you like to go in that computer store and start the research with me?" Anthony's eyes twinkled. He was very excited that they were deviating from their schedule and taking some time to learn more about his interest. Martha took her pad of paper and wrote down some of the questions she had mentioned. Then she said, "Let's go find out what we can. We are not going to buy anything today, we are just learning more about it. Okay?" Anthony nodded with a big grin across his face. It was a moment that he would remember later in life when it would be time to buy a house or a car. Martha was teaching Anthony how to approach a situation, and since they were doing it together, it became fun. She could also use the experience later as a reference. "Remember when we did the computer research? Well, buying a ten-speed bike is similar."

Learning opportunities are everywhere. You need to be aware of them, pay attention when they surface, and seize them. Martha had something to contribute. Anthony asked for information. Together they learned about the subject of computers, as well as how to approach a serious purchase, and together they created a model for information-gathering and decision-making.

Consequences and rewards

It has been said that your either motivate with a carrot or a stick, and this goes for teaching your child as well. Children respond to reinforcement, either positive or negative. If you dwell on the fact that their room is always a mess, you'll see more chaos and disorder. If you dwell on how bad their grades are, they become worse and may even fail. On the other hand, if you praise the way they look after they take a bath, they will enjoy being clean and start to bathe more often. If you focus on how well they do their math homework, they will take pride in their accuracy. Pay attention to what you say and especially *how* you say it. The volume of your words goes much farther than the actual words. Children are volume sensitive. If you say "Good job" in a low, sweet tone about their writing assignment, and fly off the handle when they drop the bowl of chocolate sauce on the floor, don't be surprised if they become more clumsy, and start "accidentally" dropping more things. You might very well be reinforcing the exact opposite of what you wish.

It would seem logical that children would continue behaviors that secure them rewards and cease those that lead to punishment, but that isn't always the case. Unfortunately, their psyches cannot always differentiate between positive and negative attention, and sometimes they will unconsciously do whatever will get them the most attention. They simply gravitate to behaviors that create the greatest response. This means that the volume of your verbal communication, the effect on their adrenal glands from the intensity of the message, and the degree of emotion all imprint on them. Your child may be seeking recognition, and if she does not receive it positively, because it is expected, or because you are too busy, then she will look for other alternatives, or negative attention. In other words, receiving no attention at all is not an option, and negative attention is better than no attention at all.

Billy and Melissa presented a classic case of sibling rivalry. Melissa was two years older, did well in school, and received lots of positive praise from her parents Joe and Liz about her grades, her friends, her music skills, and so on. The family mantra about Melissa was that she was "a pleasure." Billy, on the other hand, was labeled a "problem child" early on. He was hyperactive as a young child, and what started as cute and mischievous pranks grew into more aggressive behavior. His parents were frequently called in to the principal's office to discuss something he'd done, and as a result, he was usually in some sort of trouble. His parents were often angry or annoyed with him for some reason, whether it was throwing a baseball in the house and breaking a window or cheating on a math test.

As the years went by, Billy's behavior deteriorated. He was suspended for setting off a fire alarm, and several weeks later, his parents came home to discover that he had driven their car (he was only 14 years old at the time). They yelled, they punished, they negotiated, they even tried reasoning with him, all to no avail. To Joe and Liz, it felt like there was nothing they could do to control their son's behavior.

Joe and Liz came to see me to try to find some solutions. For the first hour, they vented their frustrations. They told me all the stories in detail, as though they needed an outside party to verify that they were living in a nightmare. When they had exhausted their repertoire of stories, they turned to me to ask how I would suggest they "fix" their son.

I asked them to tell me more about their family dynamic. Whenever they spoke about Melissa, it was in glowing tones. When they mentioned Billy, they sounded alternately frustrated, angry, and hopeless. For Melissa, they held the highest hopes. Thinking about Billy triggered only resignation. The system of consequence and reward was crystal clear. Both children had learned to live up to the roles that their parents had created for them. Melissa learned to get attention by being a "good girl," and Billy learned to get it by acting out in negative ways. How this cycle had started wasn't critical; what mattered most was that this was the paradigm they were presently living out each and every day.

Of course, this situation is by no means all Joe and Liz's fault. Having a child with behavior problems is incredibly challenging, and it can be difficult knowing what to do to get your child back on the right track. I encouraged Joe and Liz to look inward at how their reactions were perhaps reinforcing the situation. By continuing to focus on everything Melissa did right, they received positive results; by continuously focusing on everything Billy did wrong, the outcome was negative. Even the slightest shift in where they put their attention could break Billy's cycle of negative behavior/negative reward/repeated negative behavior.

Joe and Liz tried to refocus their attention regarding their son. It wasn't easy to find things to reward Billy for, but they tried to do it at least once a day. They also leveled off their anger when Billy acted out, administering whatever punishment they decided upon calmly instead of reacting with emotional extremes. Liz called me a few weeks later and told me that Billy had actually looked a little disappointed when they told him calmly that he was grounded for coming home an hour past curfew; he was ready for a high-energy blowout, and their reaction took a little of the wind out of his sails. There weren't any major miracles, but they did notice a change in the energy in their home. Billy didn't turn into an angel overnight, though he did seem less angry. He is starting to show signs of growing out of his need for negative attention.

You can't always change how your child acts or reacts, but you can shift how you contribute to the dynamic. Paying attention to where you put your energy is important, since you can be certain you will get more of whatever you dwell on. Ironically, one of the best ways to halt negative actions is to stop focusing on them.

On the other hand, adults often take for granted behaviors that are desirable. For instance, if a child makes his bed, brushes his teeth without being told, goes to bed without a fuss, or puts his toys away without being asked, parents are pleased but often don't say anything. They may think these behaviors are *normal* and therefore *expected*.

In order to reinforce desirable behaviors, you want to focus on everything your child does that is positive and self-affirming. Remembering these guidelines may help:

1. Recognize everything they do that you have requested.
2. Reinforce their progress no matter how modest.
3. Point out their positive behaviors in a loving manner.
4. Thank them for doing what you asked.
5. Tell them you appreciate their consideration or thoughtfulness.
6. Reward attitudes and behaviors that are in alignment with your values.
7. Praise them for achieving their objectives.
8. Celebrate their triumphs.

Remember, how you respond to your children does contribute to what they will or won't do in the future. If you harp on all they do wrong, they will learn that that is the best way to elicit emotional responses and recognition from you. Give them the positive reinforcement they seek when they behave as you would like, and you increase the chances that they will continue to do so.

The transfer of responsibilities

There needs to be a transfer of responsibilities with your child's growing capabilities. For instance, as children learn to cook, you allow them to participate in meal preparation. As they learn to do laundry, you include them in the process by letting them pour the soap or throw in the socks. As they learn to drive a car, you entrust them with grocery shopping. Little by little, they begin to master skills that heretofore were beyond their capability. As you do less and empower them to do more for themselves, you are demonstrating that you trust them, that you think they are capable, and that you believe in them.

Mothers have a tendency to get stuck in their previous job descriptions. They once did everything for their child; now that the child is 16, 17, or 18, they are still doing everything. I know one woman whose son, a college freshman, didn't know how to do laundry, boil an egg, open a can, make plane reservations, or balance his checkbook—all because his mother had done everything for him right up until the day he left home.

If you do everything for your child, you are infantilizing rather than empowering. When you infantilize someone, you unconsciously treat them as incompetent by doing things for them that they are fully capable of doing themselves. Of course the opposite scenario is that of latch-key kids who have to do everything for themselves even before they are mature enough. The ideal situation is to create a steady transfer of responsibilities.

It might start with teaching your child to put away his toys on his own when he is finished playing. Later it shifts to setting the table, and still later to cleaning up his room. This continues on as children learn to care for themselves gradually, leading all the way up to their most adultlike behaviors, such as driving a car, managing their finances, and making high-level decisions.

In our world, the ideal situation is to have your child become self-sufficient by the age of 21. You have officially weaned him on all levels, and he can manage and direct his own life. You are welcome to be a part of it, yet you are not required for his survival.

RESIDENT EXPERT

You are officially the "mommy," which means you become the resident expert in everything from boo-boos to broken hearts, from tutus to prom dresses, from how to ask a girl to dance to coping with wedding anxieties, and from Gerber's to how to order a pizza in under thirty minutes. You are looked to for *all* the answers.

My friend Didi remembers the moment when she first figured out her mother didn't know everything. She was 18 and had just moved into her own apartment. She felt creative one evening and decided to dye her hair, with unfortunate results. Rather than shimmery blond, she ended up with a glowing shade of green. She panicked and called her mother to ask what to do. When her mother replied that she had no idea what to do, that Didi should wait until morning to call a hairdresser, Didi was shocked. "Can't you just tell me how to fix it?" she asked with alarm.

"Didi," her mother replied with a little laugh. "I haven't the foggiest idea how to fix this! You need an expert." It was a major moment for Didi: she realized her mom wasn't the resident wizard!

Until such time when your children are old enough to realize that you are a person, just like them, they will look to you as a walking encyclopedia. After all, you know how to make medicine bearable, how to dress for all occasions, and how to make the world's greatest chocolate brownies. In a child's mind, that means you are akin to a genius.

Children take their mother's word as gospel. I heard a funny story recently about a curious little boy who asked his mother if anything at all could be flushed down the toilet (you can imagine where this story is leading . . .). His mother was preoccupied at the moment and responded flippantly, "Yes, anything can be flushed down the toilet." Two hours and one plumber later, they managed to retrieve the pile of orange rinds the boy had stuffed down there, because Mom said "anything can be flushed down the toilet"!

When your child looks to you for information, guidance, and answers, it starts a conversation. This is an opportunity to see what your child is thinking, what she's interested in, and what she is focusing on. Use those moments of natural curiosity to connect with your child. Take a moment and focus all of your attention on her. Look into her eyes, and give her your undivided attention—100 percent of you. Remember, a child's attention span is very limited compared to yours. She is naturally inquisitive, but she will only open the door to you so many times before she shuts down and decides to go elsewhere for what she needs.

When your child asks for your time, your attention, your wisdom, don't deny her. Instead, search for ways to satisfy her request, even if it may be a bit inconvenient. If you don't know the answer yourself, then make it into a project to find out the answers together. This way you show her how to go about finding answers she needs.

You might get tired of answering all those questions. You may feel as if "why" is a word you'd like to strike from the English language. Yet the amount of patience and effort it takes to respond really isn't all that great when you think how much your child will remember the time you are taking—the bits of knowledge you are imparting—and those precious moments one to one with you.

AUTHORITY FIGURE

What you say goes. The dictionary defines "authority" as "the person or entity that has the power or right to give orders and enforce obedience." Authorities are a reality that everyone must come to terms with. In the first ten years of your child's life, you are it! After that, authorities will range from teachers and bosses to the police, the President, and the IRS. Your child can learn to deal with authority figures now or later. Authorities will never go away, and no matter where children go or how big they get they will always have to deal with someone who has more authority than they do. Whatever they do, there will always be someone who has the power to give them orders. If they learn how to deal with authority from you, it will make things easier on them later on.

Joey had authority issues from the get-go. He always asked, "Why?" and "How come?" He wanted to do things his way. He hated following rules. He resisted anyone telling him what to do. His mother, Janice, was very clear with him, yet he always thought he knew better. One night, when Joey was 16, he called home, "Mom, you're not going to like this [long pause]. I'm at the police station. Can you come get me?"

Janice and her husband drove to the police station and picked him up. He had been out late drinking and walking down the street in a part of town with a curfew. Janice and I had discussed how to deal with these "life lesson" moments, so she calmly asked, "What do you think this is trying to teach you?" Joey said, "That you were right?"

Janice continued, "Joey, in a couple of years you won't have to obey me. You won't be living at home. You will be on your own, perhaps in college, perhaps with a job. The point is, right now I am your safety net. Later on, I might not always be there to bail you out. If you learn what is here for you to learn, you won't have to repeat those same lessons down the road. So you tell me, what can you learn from this experience?"

Joey thought before he answered. "That I have to play by the rules," he said somewhat glumly. (They may learn the lesson, but rarely will they like it!) "Your rules aren't that much different from theirs, I guess; so I have to follow them or else one day I'll really get busted." Janice rested her case; Joey had gotten it.

I'll talk more about discipline in chapter 5, but for now, I'll remind you that being an authority figure requires that you assume the attitude and responsibility of one. Your children will always push to see how much they can get away with—it's up to you to show them that the buck stops with you.

FRIEND

A friend is someone you choose to spend time with because you have fun together. You might go to the movies, to the mall shopping, or for a walk on the beach. You might sit in your room talking or listening to music, or play a favorite sport together. You choose activities because they are fun and enable you to be together enjoying each other's company. When your child is little, she doesn't fit easily into the category of "friend." However, as she gets older, you will have the option of playing that role in each other's lives.

Being a friend to your child is what brings the element of enjoyment to your relationship. There were so many afternoons when Jennifer and I would jump in the car and go for coffee or hang out in her room. Other times we'd go for a walk. I treasure those as some of the most valuable times we have shared. She'd tell me what was going on in her life—with her friends, or her boyfriend—and what was bothering her, and I had the privilege of relating to my daughter as a person, not only as my child. It's not always easy to be spontaneous, but if you can seize the moment, you will never regret it.

The way to be your child's friend is to treat him as you would any other friend in your life. Listen to them, make plans to do things you both enjoy, and be there for them when they need you. Laugh together, and seek out ways to develop the person-to-person connection along with the parent/child one.

There is a danger, however, of taking this aspect of your relationship too far. It's important to always remember that although you may be your child's friend, you will always be their mother first. Your child will have lots of friends throughout his or her life but only one mother, and it's essential that you do not abandon that role in favor of being popular with your child.

Margaret raised her kids in a very laid-back manner. Margaret's three daughters thought their mother was totally cool and always brought their friends around to hang out with her. The problems arose when they were in their later teens and really needed a mother figure to guide them. When they needed advice about boys, dating, sex, studying, time management, prioritizing, and managing money, they never thought to look to Margaret. After all, Margaret had been their friend and didn't seem to have a grasp on those topics. They looked to school counselors, books, magazines, TV, and the Internet for guidance and direction. This is not terrible, but it certainly is not optimal.

The transition from authority to friend can be a challenge. As your children's guide you have been there to show the way. As their friend, you are there to enjoy their company. Sometimes children want you to be their friend, and you need to do what you believe is right even if it is not popular. Friends don't impose limits or enforce consequences, and this is where the conflict can occur.

Clara and her 16-year-old daughter, Stephanie, were enjoying the day at their local craft fair. Stephanie had read about it in the paper and expressed interest, and Clara suggested they go together. As they walked amongst the handmade candles and carved wooden objects, they chatted about clothes, the new boy in school Stephanie thought was cute, and a television sitcom they both watched regularly. It was a really fun day, and at one point Stephanie linked her arm through her mother's and remarked how much she liked "hanging out" with her. Clara was delighted that her daughter thought of her as a friend, in addition to her mother.

That night, Stephanie went out with her friends from school and came home drunk. Clara was angry, and when she demanded an explanation from Stephanie, her daughter replied, "Chill out, Mom. You were so cool today—now you're going to hassle me and be all motherly and stuff?"

"You bet I am!" Clara responded.

The next morning, Clara had a talk with Stephanie about boundaries. She explained that although Stephanie could look to her as a friend, she could not abuse that aspect of their relationship and deny her "daughter" role. Clara said that she could, of course, be her daughter's friend, but she would always be her mother first and foremost. Stephanie admitted she had pushed too far the night before, assuming that Clara would let her behavior slide based on how "cool" her mom had been acting all day.

It's important to clearly mark out the parameters of your "friend" moments. It's also helpful for you to remember not to cross the line yourself by trying to make your child *your* friend. Confiding about your personal adult issues or treating your child like your peer only further blurs the boundaries. If you want advice or someone to confide in, it is better to seek out someone on your own level, rather than setting up a dynamic in which you and your child are equals.

It's not easy to find the balance between the roles of authority figure and friend, but with practice, you can strike it. Remember to give clear signals to your child about what you expect, and how far you are willing to let your role as "friend" stretch you.

SOURCE OF LOVE

You teach your children the meaning of love. You teach them how to give and receive love. You make it safe for them to open their hearts and connect with another. If they haven't learned to love from you, it will be difficult for them to love another. If they haven't learned how to receive love from you, then they may be closed off to others. You are the wellspring of love—you convey the essence of loving and being loved to your child.

Love is not something you teach by telling; it is something you show by doing. Love is the look in your eye, the touch of your hand, the music in your laughter, the flavor of your mashed potatoes, the blotting of a tear. It comes from who you are, shines from your being, and is translated into little acts in everything you do. Love is the fertile soil from which all good things blossom. Love is your ultimate gift to your child . . . that no matter what happens in life, you will always love them.

Mothering is the ultimate form of multitasking. You'll find that your job has many dimensions to it, and that it may be challenging to fulfill all the roles asked of you. Take each day as it comes, and soon enough you will learn which role you need to play for your child at what time. The key to success in any job is flexibility, and that was never truer for any job than that of being a mother!

$\mathcal{T}r u t h$ #4

CHILDREN BLOSSOM WHEN YOU HONOR THEIR ESSENCE

Nurturing children includes supporting what is unique and special about them.

Your children are not your children.
They are the sons and daughters of Life's
  longing for itself.
They come through you but not from you,
And though they are with you yet they belong
  not to you.
You may give them your love but not your
  thoughts.
For they have their own thoughts.
You may house their bodies but not their
  souls,

For their souls dwell in the house of tomorrow,
Which you cannot visit, not even in your
    dreams.
You may strive to be like them, but seek not
    to make them like you.
For life goes not backward nor tarries with
    yesterday.
You are the bows from which your children as
    living arrows are sent forth.

THE PROPHET

KAHLIL GIBRAN

Within each of us is an essence—some call it spirit, others call it soul, being, or "self." Regardless of what you call it, each of us has an essence that is unique unto us. One's essence is something beyond brain, flesh, bone, or blood type. It exists on levels far deeper than our job descriptions, or our marital status, or even our state of physical health. The essence of a human being is the nonphysical, intangible consciousness that simply *is*. It houses what we know and love, what we sense and what we cherish. It is who we are at our innermost core.

Children are born with an essence that is unique unto them—an essence that is deep, rare, and very precious. Their essence is special and theirs alone. Part of your challenge as a mother is connecting with that essence, discovering *who* your child is, and assisting her in developing her sense of self in the world. This is one of the most sacred duties of motherhood. The most valuable gift you can give your child is to pay attention, to notice and to help her discover her essence, and to honor it through support and encouragement. Even if it is very different from your own, and especially if it is not what you might have envisioned.

Think of it this way: within each child is a tiny seed. That seed is the origin of who she is. With careful tending—attention, love, nurturing—that seed can one day grow into the bloom it is meant to be. Ignore that seed—try to change it, deny it sunlight and nutrients—and it may never blossom into its full true potential. You are the one who can nurture it and get it to grow. If you pay attention, you can discover the seedling within your child. You can give it what it needs to thrive, so that one day your child will be prepared to take on the world with whatever it has to offer and with all its challenges.

A mother's impact on her child's psyche and self-esteem can be considerable. I remember feeling overwhelmed when I first had Jennifer—how could I possibly give my child everything she needed to grow into a psychologically, spiritually, and emotionally healthy adult? How could I prevent her from one day lying on a therapist's couch complaining about how I had ruined her self-esteem? Would she one day blame me for not giving her all the tools she needed to thrive? It was unsettling to me to imagine that I could have such a profound impact on the spiritual development of another human being.

Though I held this thought in the back of my mind, the pressure looming over me wore off once I was involved in the actual process of raising Jennifer. I thought less about all that could go wrong and instead tried to focus more on what I could do well—how I could give that little essence inside her all the love and care it deserved so that she could one day grow into the incredible woman she has now become. I always wonder what I might have done better. However, when I look at her and see how confident, articulate, and capable she is, I guess I must have done something right.

In order to honor your child's essence, you must go beneath the persona of your child and find the true essence that dwells within your little one. It is with *you* that your child needs to be free to discover who he is. It all begins in those first few years, when he is discovering the world and his place within it. The more you encourage him to honor the sacred and unique parts of himself, the easier it will be for him to fully become who he is. The more you allow him to be himself and not who you would like him to be, the more you equip him to deal effectively with the world, with its challenges, opportunities, setbacks, and victories.

Recognizing the Essence of Your Child

A kiss from my mother made me a painter.   BENJAMIN WEST

Recognizing the essence of your child is really all about finding out what matters to him. In the first few years his individual personality begins to emerge, and with your assistance, the little sparks of interest, enthusiasm, and passion within him light his path to a well-developed sense of self. It's not really about whether he likes peas or chicken, or whether he feels happier in blue or red. It's not even about the little character traits he develops. It's about what lies beneath that: what makes him laugh, what creates his delight, what gifts he offers to the world, what makes him who he is.

What matters to children? What makes their eyes light up? What makes them flush with excitement, or propels them into action? What do they enjoy? In what areas do they appear to have innate, natural ability? What are their talents? What are their gifts? What makes them special? What makes them unique?

If you watch closely for clues, their twinkles will light the way. You can catch a glimpse of their passion if you pay close attention. It is fleeting, here and then gone. The signals will become clear to you if you are watching, listening and noticing what they are unconsciously showing you. If you are willing to observe them as different from you, the rest of your family, your community, and friends, children will let you see who they are on the inside . . . in their heart . . . in their spirit . . . in their essence.

I have a soft spot for heartwarming commercials, including a series of commercials for an online toy retailer that speaks to the value of recognizing your child's essence. In one, a child is sitting at an adult dinner party, wholly absorbed in building a house out of his asparagus. His mother catches sight of him doing this and sees his interest in building things. Of course she goes online and purchases a Lego set for him to encourage him in something he enjoys. The child is delighted and the mother is happy knowing she recognized the spark behind her child's eyes. If this scenario were real, the boy might not necessarily grow up to be an architect, engineer, or construction worker, but he would have a clear sense that his interests matter.

How do you recognize the essence of your child? It begins with the very simple step of observation. Watch what he does; listen to what he says. Pay attention to the clues he is giving you. When Diana's son Marcus repeatedly talked about his drama class in school, Diana clued in and started taking Marcus to see plays. Marcus was awed each and every time the curtain went up. Since he is still only 16 years old, Diana doesn't know whether he will eventually make a lifetime commitment to acting, directing, or set design, but what really matters is that his creative spirit has been encouraged.

Pay attention to how your child reacts in different situations. Sharla's daughter Lauren was quiet and serious. Sharla tried to encourage her to go out and play, to have fun with her friends. Instead Lauren preferred to stay in her room and read. Sharla insisted Lauren go to a social at their church, at which Sharla was acting as a chaperone. Instead of having fun, Lauren looked uncomfortable all evening.

Sharla realized she'd assumed Lauren just needed a little push to have some fun, when what Lauren really needed was for her mother to notice that their definitions of fun were different. Lauren loved her books, and was far happier reading Charlotte Brontë than dancing to Ricky Martin. Lauren's essence was more aligned with intellectual pursuits than with parties, and once Sharla recognized that, she was able to nurture that part of her intelligent, well-read daughter. She stopped asking Lauren why she didn't go out and have fun, and started asking about the latest book she was reading.

Believe in children's innate ability to know what they truly want. If you always come from the position that you are older, wiser, more experienced, then you disallow your child the chance to connect with what they inherently know about themselves. I was once standing at a concession stand at a concert and heard a woman ask her son what he wanted. He said, "popcorn."

"No, you don't want popcorn," she said. "It's greasy. Don't you want a pretzel?"

The kid looked confused; he'd already told her what he wanted. The woman was not really saying, "what do you want?" but rather, "here's what you should want." It's not that this child's essence was wrapped around popcorn or a pretzel, but his innate ability to choose what he wanted was being challenged.

Make a pact with yourself to never consciously stifle your child's essence, and you will be amazed at how clearly it becomes apparent to you. If you commit to keeping the light in her eyes alive, you will automatically seek out ways to keep it aglow. Focus on and nurture who she is, and her seeds of self will grow abundantly.

RECOGNIZE YOUR CHILD'S GIFTS
Every child has a gift. It could be athletic, mechanical, a knack with numbers, musical abilities, physical attractiveness, an ability to connect with people, an aesthetic sense, a flare for foreign languages, or the ability to make people laugh. Part of your task as a mother is discovering your child's gifts. Gifts are not always obvious, especially if you are looking through the prism of your own experiences. In order to see your child's gifts, you need to observe without bias. This means that you must set aside your own preconceived notions of what he or she can and can't do, should or shouldn't be able to do. It

means that you must see the innate gifts for what they are, not what you think they should be.

Tiger Woods came from a family that played golf, but not world-class championship golf. Shannon Miller came from a family that supported her gymnastics, but her parents were not gymnasts themselves. Nobel Prize winners did not receive their prizes because of their parents' genes, nor did world leaders become elected because leadership ran in the family.

Jasmine had a flair for fashion. She knew what colors, textures, and styles naturally went together. She had never studied fashion, yet ever since she was a little child, she knew how to put together a look. Her mother had never been trendy or fashionable. Her father was very traditional in his dress. She was an only child, so she hadn't learned this from her siblings. Call it a knack, an intuition, or a gift, Jasmine had it. She knew what looked good, she trusted herself, and anyone who would let her take charge had an almost instant makeover. Her mother continually scratched her head when she saw Jasmine doing someone's hair, makeup, or clothing. It just didn't make sense.

"Where that child got that ability is a mystery to me," she would say.

I would gently remind her again and again: "It's a gift. That's all!"

What are your child's gifts? What does she say or do that makes her stand out? What are you doing to enhance and support those gifts?

Nurturing Your Child's Essence

Children are likely to live up to what you believe of them.

LADY BIRD JOHNSON

Nurturing your child's essence is the key to building self-esteem. The world may imprint on children as they go through life, but the root of their self-esteem begins with whoever fills the role of primary caretaker. Shouldering responsibility for building and fostering your child's self-esteem may seem like a big job, but it need not be daunting if you remember that those who are cherished and honored for who they are tend to feel good about themselves.

Having self-esteem means being capable of meeting life's challenges and knowing you are worthy of happiness. It is the basis on which we measure our worth, and the most important building block in the foundation of our psyches. If you want to develop your child's self-esteem, you'll need to practice a variation of the golden rule: **Do unto your children as you would like them to do unto themselves.**

In other words, your child learns from you how he deserves to be treated. If you respect his needs, he learns to respect them also. If you tell and show him often that he is loved, he will learn to treat himself with love. If you honor your commitments to him, he will learn to honor his commitments to himself. Think of your child as a mini-mirror that reflects inward the messages and cues he receives from you.

Children internalize your beliefs about them, then adopt them as their own. There is a wonderful book by Laurie Beth Jones called *The Power of Positive Prophecy* that talks about how highly successful people like Jackie Joyner Kersey grew into the recordbreakers they are because of the positive prophecies their families created for them. If you believe your children can do anything, chances are they will. If you believe they are worthy of love, they will believe it too. If you treat them as deserving of respect, they will treat themselves respectfully.

I know a man who innately believes that everything in his life will work out all right. He leads a stress-free life, not because he does not have large commitments (he is a lawyer in a large firm, financially supports a family of five, and actively volunteers for two major non-profit organizations), but because he refuses to stress about them. He does what he can do and rarely seems frazzled or worried when I asked him how he manages. He once told me it was because he really saw no reason to get stressed out; he knew everything would work out in the end. He thought, "Why worry?"

It wasn't until I met this man's parents a few years ago that it became clear to me where his attitude came from. Both his parents were in their eighties and still believed their son could do absolutely anything. They had told him his whole life that he could be, do, or have anything he set his mind to, and that belief became part of his emotional and psychological tapestry. He lived up to the prophecy his family created for him because they (and in turn, he) completely believed that it was true.

There are many ways you can help develop and nurture your

child's sense of self-esteem. The following are a few ideas to get you started:

Ten Things You Can Do to Develop Children's Self-Esteem

1. Show your love every day in clear demonstrable ways. For example, make a special food they like, or show up for their athletic event even though you're busy. These actions show them that they are worthy of love, and reinforce the idea that they deserve it.

2. Sincerely tell children that you love them at least once a day. Hearing it directly and clearly ensures that they get the message.

3. Assist them in setting mini-goals and help them succeed. Accomplishment makes people feel good about themselves. It will give your child reasons to be proud.

4. Reinforce everything positive; notice what they've done right. This keeps your—and their—focus on what they do well, rather than on what they don't.

5. Have them see the opportunity to learn from each situation. When things go wrong, seeking out the lessons to be learned makes the overall experience less of a "failure" in their eyes. The less they see themselves as failing, the less they will beat themselves up.

6. Make promises you can deliver; then always make good on your promises. Keeping your promises reinforces that your child matters. Broken promises signal that they are not a priority.

7. Provide structure—set clear, fair limits and expectations and adhere to them. When they know the rules, they can succeed by following them. Mixed signals lead to confusion and doubt about what they are supposed to do.

8. Listen to what they have to say. Listening shows them that what they have to say is of value.

9. Reward behaviors that you want to see more of. Celebrate their victories. They need to feel the delight of succeeding so they can be motivated to keep striving.

10. Love them unconditionally, and process your own issues elsewhere. Children need to know you love them no matter what they do. When they know they are loved for themselves, regardless of what they do, they will enter the world proud to be who they are.

WHEN YOUR CHILD IS DIFFERENT FROM YOU

Not every mother nurtures her child's essence. Many have hopes, agendas, and even specific plans that their children are supposed to fulfill. Sometimes these expectations are tangible and conscious: some want them to follow in the family footsteps, on a path that may already be deeply etched. They are slated to go to the same university as their parents and grandparents, programmed to go into the same profession or take over the family business. They are expected to have the same strengths and weaknesses that have run in the family genes for generations.

Other times the expectations are unconscious. A father who loves fishing may wish for a son to fish with him, and may not consider that his child would rather be playing street hockey. A mother who loves ballet may automatically enroll her daughter in class, assuming she will respond to dance with the same enthusiasm. Liberal parents might expect their child to automatically espouse the same social consciousness with which they were raised. Professional women often assume their daughters will be ambitious like they are. Mothers who love to cook assume they will have children who love to create in the kitchen.

When we feel pride in our children—when their essence is aligned with what we hoped they would be—honoring them seems to come naturally. Natasha, a very earthy woman who believed strongly in animal rights, never felt a moment's anxiety about her daughter Maia, who chose to become a vegetarian like Natasha at a very early age. She felt in alignment with her daughter and found it easy to encourage her to blossom.

On the other hand, it is something entirely different to be supportive when they diverge from what you believe your child should be. The biggest obstacle many parents face is allowing a child's essence to emerge if it differs from what they envisioned. It can be challenging to remember that your child is a being unto himself, and not merely a blank screen onto which you can project your expectations or even your own unfulfilled dreams.

There are so many sad stories of mothers who force their children into show business or modeling because that is what they always dreamed of doing themselves. Parents who were denied certain opportunities, like summer camp, may force them upon their child, even if their child does not necessarily express an interest. When children become an outlet for living out our unlived dreams, they are cheated of the opportunity to live their own dreams. They are too busy fulfilling our fantasies to create and experience their own. It is hard to honor your child's true essence if it is eclipsed by your desire for her to be what you want her to be.

It would be nice to think that our children will follow in our finest footsteps. Regardless of our wishes, hopes, aspirations, and yearnings, however, our children do not always fulfill our expectations. There is no guarantee that your child will turn out like you, or as you might wish. It is in this area that you will be called upon to stretch your realm of possibilities for the sake of your child.

Sheila had been a gymnast as a teen and later went on to be a professional gymnastics coach. She married Joe, an athlete who played ball, ran, and skied. Together they were extremely active, spending weekends in the outdoors hiking, biking, and camping. Their lifestyle revolved around physical activity. The challenge for Sheila was understanding and nurturing the essence of Stan, a son who had absolutely no interest in athletics.

Sheila admitted that she had always envisioned training her child in a sport, perhaps even urging him on to the Olympics. That fit her picture of the son she was "supposed to" have. Clearly, nature and genes had other plans, and she had a son who was more interested in computers than the great outdoors.

Stan was definitely a computer nerd. By the time he was five, he was using a mouse; at the age of seven, his little fingers were dancing across the keyboard. He learned games in a matter of minutes. By the time he was ten, he was the resident wizard in his neighborhood. He could navigate the Internet like a pro, and even helped Joe create a spreadsheet for the family's finances.

At first, Sheila joked that there had been a mix-up at the hospital nursery since Stan didn't match the rest of his family. When everyone wanted to go camping, Stan wanted to stay indoors and surf the

Web. He couldn't catch or throw a ball very far, but he could install, configure, and repair most problems on any PC.

Sheila, thankfully, was someone with a good deal of awareness, and she recognized that she had the power to encourage Stan in what he loved, or squelch that passion through disinterest or discouragement. She chose the former and dedicated herself to learning about Stan's interest so that she could share it with him. Sheila surprised Stan for his thirteenth birthday by enrolling him in computer camp rather than the sports camp he had attended the previous two summers. He was thrilled!

Mary Beth was the CEO of a large textile company. She had worked her way up the ladder from secretary to CEO in twenty years, and had no plans to stop. Mary Beth wanted to be on the board of a Fortune 500 company and dedicated much of her efforts to making that happen.

As fate would have it, Mary Beth's daughter Susie was more interested in going to the mall than in charting her life's ambitions. As serious and work-oriented as Mary Beth was, Susie was equally cavalier and laid back. "Chill, Mom" was a favorite refrain.

On the one hand, Mary Beth desperately wished her daughter had inherited some of her drive. She believed in her bones that the motivation to succeed was the greatest gift a person could possess. On the other hand, she saw a lightness in Susie that she had always wished she had. It was a complex psychological web that Mary Beth worked through when she realized that she needed to foster Susie's nature even though she might feel conflicted about it.

Planes fascinated Elena's daughter Dallas. From the time she was a tiny child, every flying object she saw mesmerized her. When she was five, she flew to Hawaii with her family. The pilot invited her into the cockpit to see the instruments. She knew at that moment that this was for her. She started to collect miniature planes, and she watched every TV special about aviation. Elena was afraid of heights and didn't like to fly. The thought of Dallas becoming a pilot was totally beyond her comprehension.

It took all of Elena's willpower to hold back her fears about aviation, and the idea of her daughter going into this risky field. She knew, however, that her fears would not be helpful to her daughter. Elena had to process her concerns and worries on her own and find a way to support Dallas in pursuing her dream. She did all she could to honor Dallas, even though her passion was dramatically different from what Elena might have wished for her daughter.

For Sheila, Mary Beth, and Elena the path of motherhood was certainly not easy. Each had to bond with her child, connect with her essence, then pay attention, listen, and support her child's proclivity even though she had difficulty relating to it. In each instance, the process was formidable, but it was worth it. Rather than forcing a round peg into a square hole, they were nurturing an essence they couldn't identify with, and by doing so, allowing their children to blossom into who they were meant to be.

If your child is different from you, ask yourself how willing you are to encourage him in his own development. Do you hold him back because he is not like you, or because he doesn't fit your idea of what your child should be like? Can you put your own expectations aside and recognize that one of your responsibilities as a mother is to support and nurture all his best facets, regardless of whether they fit with your agenda?

Connecting with Your Child

The walks and talks we have with our two-year-olds in red boots have a great deal to do with the values they will cherish as adults.

EDITH F. HUNTER

I recently saw a billboard in New York with a picture of a young teen on it. The ad's caption said, "If only children came with instructions." Written on the child's arm was "Stay involved in my life."

The connection you have with your child is one of the best ways you can ensure your child stays rooted in his or her essence and doesn't stray too far. It is when children lose their sense of self that they get involved with drugs and seek other damaging ways to feel fulfilled. Of course, there is no guarantee that if you stay connected to them they will turn out perfectly. No one can guarantee that. But I can promise that your child will be more likely to blossom if she is connected both to you and to her essence.

There is no set formula for staying connected to your child. However, if you do your best, you will form a strong bond that will survive the wear and tear of difficult times. Check out the following list:

Ways to stay connected to children

1. Make time for them in their chosen activities and show them they are important to you.
2. When they speak, listen to everything they are saying.
3. Be interested in what they care about.
4. Carve out time to be with them.
5. Allow them to teach you.
6. When they tell you potentially alarming information, don't overreact.
7. When they express enthusiasm, interest, and excitement, fuel the flame.
8. Suspend judgment when they stretch outside your comfort zone.
9. Guidance requires structure, discipline and wisdom.
10. Show up for the moments that matter.

*Make time for them, to show them that
they are important to you.*

With all the tasks you must fulfill as a mother, it is easy to understand why your child might feel like another "to do" in your already busy schedule. However, time to connect on a regular basis is to a child what sunlight is to plants. Never assume that children know you love them. They need to be told and shown frequently. Never assume that children automatically know they are special to you.

Even if you are busy—even if you have the biggest presentation of your life, if the boiler broke for the third time this year, if you have social obligations—remember that your children only have one mother, you. They need your love and your assurance that they are important to you. Remember to give them that gift often.

Listen when they speak.

If you want children to feel insignificant, interrupt them every time they speak to you. If you want them to feel special, pay attention to what they have to say. Stop what you are doing, look them in the eye, and give them 100 percent of your attention. It doesn't have to last for long . . . a few moments, and they will be satisfied. Give them your complete attention even if only for the connection they deserve.

Children need to know that what they say is important, so that they can develop a healthy sense of self-esteem. It's easy to give them your ear, and how better to bond with anyone than to *really* listen to them?

Be interested in what they care about.

Their interests are not your interests. You are not learning to multiply, skateboard, or play T-ball. It's all too easy to be uninterested or preoccupied with your own concerns. However, it is a genuine acknowledgment for you to be sincerely interested in their friends, studies, games, and hobbies. They will shine as soon as you take an interest in whatever they are into.

It helps to ask them questions about their friends, studies, sports, teachers, and hobbies. When you ask questions, you show that you are interested. Don't assume that if they have something to tell you, they will be forthcoming. Children will often hang back waiting for an invitation to disclose information. They might assume that you are either not interested or too busy. They may have tried in the past to tell you something about their interests, and if you were distracted, they may have decided that you don't really care. Ask, listen, and show you're interested in their world.

Sidney had zero interest in comic books until her son Zack became an avid collector. It was important to her to stay involved in Zack's life. She started asking him about the different books he was buying and even agreed to take him to a comic book convention sixty miles away. One day when they were on a plane together, Sidney asked Zack if she could read one of his comic books. He looked at her, shocked, replied, "Sure Mom," and handed her one he felt she could grasp. Zack felt her interest in his passion, and as a result, Sidney was the first person he called to share the news that he'd won a coveted comic book online. It was a great bonding moment between a mother and son who might have missed out had Sidney not taken an interest in her son's hobby.

Carve out time to be with them.

There is never enough time for children. It may appear as if the more you give, the more they want. There is, however, a day when all of this changes. There will be a day when they stop asking for your time. There will also be a day when they are too busy to find time for *you*.

In order for your child to feel special, you must *carve* out time to spend together. It might be a walk at sunset that you take together each day, or a week in the mountains every August. It could be cooking Sunday brunch together, fishing at the lake, time at the beach, golf, tennis, backpacking, or going camping. It means that you look at your calendar and find time for the two of you. You find time away from the phones, faxes, e-mail, doorbell, TV, stereo, and your various commitments, and you make a promise. No one gets to elbow in on the union between the two of you. Call it relationship building, mom and kid time, or sacred seconds, but regardless of what you call it, it should be nonnegotiable. Whatever fits with your lifestyle, budget, and shared preferences is what you should choose. Put your child at the center of your life, let her feel special, and do something together just for the sheer fun of it. Enjoy who she is and share a precious moment. Before you know it, such chances will be gone.

Allow them to teach you.

You are the mother. You have been there, done that. You are older, and the general assumption is that children will learn from you, not you from them. Turn the tables, and allow them to be your teacher. Give them the opportunity to teach you something you don't know.

Maddie had been a diehard skier since she was a young girl, and taught her daughter to ski when she was old enough. Lisa became an expert skier and later fell in love with snowboarding. Lisa was 11 when she tried to convince Maddie to let her show her how to snowboard. Maddie was dubious; she didn't relish the idea of landing on her bottom in the snow (which seemed to be a big part of what snowboarding was about), but Lisa was so excited and persistent that she agreed to try.

Lisa walked Maddie through putting on all the unfamiliar gear, then took her mother to the bunny slope. As she had foreseen, Maddie spent the rest of the day falling not only on her derriere, but on her face as well. She was sore and more than just a little bruised. But the look of excitement on Lisa's face when her mother snowboarded twenty feet made up for it. It was evident to Maddie how much of a lift Lisa got from being the one who could teach her mom something, instead of it being the familiar other way around.

When you allow children to teach you, you let them try on the role of "resident expert" for a while. They experience a sense of pride in what they can do and in their ability to show you something that you might not have known had it not been for them.

When they tell you potentially alarming information, don't overreact.

Children like to see your reactions. It seems to be a universal truth in most cultures. Be aware and be ready. So when they tell you about friends ditching school, smoking pot, having sex or anything else that might make your hair stand on end, know that they are testing you. They want to see if you will react, and how you will react. They want to know if you can "take it." If you go ballistic and freak out, they will decide that you can't handle it, and they will withhold potentially shocking news from your naïve and fragile ears. If you breathe, listen, and say, "what else?" they will intuit that you are able to handle their secrets and will be much more likely to be open with you in the future. If they tell you information that is antithetical to your values, make it known at the right moment—don't slam the door!

Andrea's daughter Cindy loved to try to shock her mother with stories about her friend Janice, who slept around. She often relayed stories that made Andrea's toes curl, but Andrea refused to crack. She responded calmly each time with an expression of compassion for Janice, and strong concern that Janice might get herself into trouble. Andrea suspected her daughter was engaging in similar behaviors, but she knew Cindy would never confide in her if she judged her friend harshly. Andrea made it clear that she did not condone these behaviors, but she did not overreact.

When Cindy was 17, she got pregnant. She chose to go to her mother and tell her, and together they were able to decide the best course of action. Andrea was, of course, deeply concerned about her daughter, but she was grateful that Cindy felt comfortable enough to confide in her rather than turning to strangers. Andrea knew then that she had made the right choice in not letting Cindy's stories about Janice throw her over the edge. If she had, her daughter would never have trusted her enough to come to her with such a serious challenge.

When they express enthusiasm, interest,
and excitement, fuel the flame.

Match their energy. When children show you that they are excited about something, share the joy. Fuel their fire. Show them that their excitement is yours also. Let them see the light in your eyes. Let them see your enthusiasm and delight in their victories. Allow them to see that their wins are your wins.

Matt loved playing with his Game Boy. He played with it day and night. Joyce, his mother, would sigh, take a deep breath, and bite her tongue. She had little tolerance for "that thing," as she called it. One day, Matt came running into Joyce's study saying, "I did it, I did it, Mom, I finally did it!" Joyce, taken aback, replied, "You did what,

Matt?" "I broke the record. I did the game faster than anyone my age has ever done it! Mom, isn't that great?" Joyce had to find the enthusiasm that she clearly lacked. It was difficult for her to get excited about "that thing," but she was personally thrilled by his joy at having accomplished an important goal. Matching energy sometimes requires that you look past the form (Game Boy) of an accomplishment and focus on its substance (Matt's achievement of a desired goal).

Suspend judgment when they stretch
outside your comfort zone.

It's one of the most difficult things to do, but if you can set aside your judgments in order to permit your children some room for experimentation, it really can create a zone of negotiation. Your children will experiment. They will question authority. They will challenge the status quo. They will take reality as it has been presented and see if it holds true for them. If you can permit them some space to find their own definition of themselves within all that they have been told, they will one day be very grateful.

Eliza's son Jeremy turned "Goth" when he was 14. (If you don't know what "Goth" is, it's short for gothic, and means dressing all in black and looking like a vampire.) Eliza was horrified to watch her adorable son transform into Dracula; it certainly didn't fit in at the tennis club where she and her family belonged. Though she was admittedly embarrassed when Jeremy showed up at a barbeque at their club in full Goth attire, she repeatedly reminded herself that experimenting was part of growing up. He wasn't doing anything to hurt himself, like drugs, piercing, or hanging out with dangerous kids. She decided to ride it out, secretly praying Jeremy would get over it but publicly supporting him however he chose to visually express himself.

Jeremy outgrew his "Goth" look within four months and moved on to become a regular jock. Eliza isn't sure what phase will come next, but whatever it is, Jeremy will one day thank his mother for allowing him to try on different personas while he figured out who he was.

Guidance requires structure, discipline, and wisdom.
Your children will no doubt push you to the limit. Realize that they require your unconditional commitment to them throughout it all. You may disapprove, and you may withdraw, but underneath it all, they want to know that you will never abandon them. See in your heart if you can love them when they deviate from the path that you have outlined for them. See if you can support them even when they listen to a different drummer. Find out where you can bend, and be clear where your breaking points are.

I have heard the words "Choose your battles" in relation to raising teens for years. When I actually had one I understood what those words meant. If you don't choose your battles, you can end up arguing around the clock about everything. You want to assess what is "small stuff," as Richard Carlson calls it, and what is big stuff. For instance, maybe you can handle pierced ears but not a pierced nose. Maybe you can deal with bleached blond hair but not green or blue. You might agree to one TV show per school night, but that's where you draw the line. Having clear and reasonable boundaries and agreements helps to provide structure for your child without making you unapproachable.

When Jennifer, my daughter, conducted focus groups with teens for *If High School is a Game, Here's How to Break the Rules: A Cutting Edge Guide to Becoming Yourself*, she found that most teens and preteens said that they couldn't talk to their parents. They also stated that because of that they often lie and tell their parents what they think they want to hear as opposed to the truth. This was alarming to me, but as Jennifer explained it, "They test the waters. If their parents overreact to what they say, they stop talking." The explanation sounded disturbing, yet reasonable. Ask yourself where you draw the line. When do you listen without reacting and when do you look horror-stricken? How do you get your values and expectations across to children without having them think, "I can't tell her anything"? Here are some questions to ask yourself to illuminate the process:

1. What is your preferred outcome in this situation?
2. What response from you will produce that outcome?
3. What is your child expecting?
4. What approach will enable you to get your point across?
5. What can you do to stay connected to your child and let him or her know your concerns?

Show up for the moments that matter.
In my seminars I hear many stories of people who were deeply scarred emotionally when a parent couldn't be there for an important

moment in their lives. It's something children—and adults—never forget.

A client once told me she would never forget the time that her father didn't come to her piano recital. He had scheduled a business meeting out of town that same week and wouldn't have been able to gracefully get out of it. She felt sad and knew that she would get over it. Nonetheless, it always stayed with her.

As best you can, be there for the big moments: the birthdays, the graduations, the day they are hired for their first job. Rejoice with them when they tell you about a big success they have been striving for, and show up to hold them when their heart is broken. Be there in their moments of struggle to offer support, especially when they don't ask for it. Don't assume that if children don't ask for your help, they don't need or want your love.

Your child needs you to be the one who encourages him to bring his inner world to life. Beneath all he says and does lies a spirit just waiting to be discovered. Pay attention to, honor, and nurture the essence of the child you are blessed to guide on his path. You will be amazed at how he blossoms when you do.

$Truth$ #5

LOVE SHOWS UP IN
MANY DIFFERENT FORMS

*Your specific expression of love will change according to what
your child needs at the time.*

Children Learn What They Live

*If children live with criticism, they learn to
condemn.*
*If children live with hostility, they learn to
fight.*
*If children live with fear, they learn to be
apprehensive.*
*If children live with pity, they learn to feel
sorry for themselves.*
*If children live with ridicule, they learn to
feel shy.*

If children live with jealousy, they learn to feel envy.

If children live with shame, they learn to feel guilty.

If children live with encouragement, they learn confidence.

If children live with tolerance, they learn patience.

If children live with praise, they learn appreciation.

If children live with acceptance, they learn to love.

If children live with approval, they learn to like themselves.

If children live with recognition, they learn it is good to have a goal.

If children live with sharing, they learn generosity.

If children live with honesty, they learn truthfulness.

If children live with fairness, they learn justice.

If children live with kindness and consideration, they learn respect.

If children live with security, they learn to have faith in themselves and in those about them.

$\mathcal{L}$ove is traditionally thought of in terms of lullabies, delicious baked goodies warm from the kitchen, hugs and cuddles, laughter, presents wrapped up in colorful packages, and lots of encouragement and support from someone who is there when you most need them. Each one of us has ideas, images, and associations about the way motherly love is supposed to look. For the majority of people, it probably resembles one of those endearing paintings by Mary Cassatt, the scent of brownies baking in the kitchen, the sound of Irish lullabies crooned in soft melodic tones. It could be watching *The Wizard of Oz* on your mother's lap, the taste of ice cream and chocolate chip cookies, or the feel of that soft hand caressing your forehead as you drift off into dreamland. These sepia-toned associations of motherhood transport us wistfully to a place of safety, comfort, and warm fuzzy connections.

Is that the entire picture? Is a mother's love always and only patient and kind? Or is there more to it than that?

Love has many different faces. As a mother, the love you extend to your child must go beyond the one-dimensional level I just described. One moment might call for love to show up as humor, such as when your child needs a little cheering up after a setback; another may require that you express your love in the form of discipline. Sometimes love shows up as the rosy glow I described, but at other times it is about a broader range of human emotions and needs: it reaches into the realms of communication, support, boundary setting, and, ultimately, letting go.

The mission of motherhood is to raise healthy, happy, successful, and socially responsible adults. The task is to respond appropriately to each situation so that your child's self-esteem is preserved, so that they grow to become balanced, caring, and capable. And so your expression of love may need to take many different forms, so that you can give to your child what he or she needs at the time. It will be your lifelong work as a mother to determine the face of love your child needs at every moment and to do your best to provide that.

Each child is unique. Each situation is different. When your daughter wasn't invited to the birthday party of one of her friends, it's the moment to commiserate with her. When your son wants to quit softball because he didn't get to play, it's time to encourage him to stick with it. When children feel confused about what course to take, it's time to ask them questions and help them make choices and solve their own problems. When children feel hopeless and want to give up, it's time to reinforce their strong qualities and tell them you will never stop loving them. When your child is disrespectful and cruel, it might be time to enforce tough love. Knowing what to do and when is just something you learn as you go along.

Communication Is Love

To talk to a child, to fascinate him, is much more difficult than to win an electoral victory. But it is more rewarding. COLETTE

One of the major keys that opens the door between you and your child is communication. Communication creates a safety zone in which your child can relate to you. Ideally, it means saying and showing what you mean in a manner that is clear, and listening to what your child is saying. Just as with your adult relationships, this kind of exchange is what keeps you and your child connected and creates a flow between you that encourages learning and understanding—for both of you.

Robyn grew up in a house where she felt, even as a young child, that she was pretty much ignored. Her mother was often preoccupied, and as a result she had little patience to hear what her daughter was saying. Robyn remembers desperately wanting her mother to buy the family a new kind of orange juice she had tasted at school and liked. She asked her mother to please get it the next time she went grocery shopping, but her mother barely listened to her request and of course came home with the same old kind of juice. Being naturally creative, Robyn made up a song about why she wanted this new juice, which she rehearsed over and over before performing it for her mother. Her mother was unable to recognize the great lengths Robyn had gone to in order to get her attention, and Robyn never did get her juice. The sad part of this story is imagining the struggle Robyn probably had to endure to get her mother's attention about life issues that were of more consequence than the kind of juice that was in the fridge.

Robyn translated this unconscious message in her child mind to "my mommy doesn't care about me." It took many years for Robyn to sort this out in her adult life, and she is now consciously making efforts to listen to and communicate clearly with her own children.

THE POWER OF LISTENING

Children who are listened to feel loved: it's that simple. That's not all there is to loving them, but listening goes a long way. It shows them that you truly care what they think, feel, want, and have to say. Asked with tenderness, "How are you?" is among the most precious phrases a child can hear.

When children sense they are not being heard, they typically shut down or withdraw. On the other hand, when they sense they have the attention of their caregivers when they speak, they learn that what they have to say is worthwhile and that it is safe to express themselves. Active listening also encourages a system of reciprocity: if you listen to them, they are far more likely to listen to you.

Listening does not come naturally to everyone; often it takes effort and practice. It can sometimes be easier to dismiss what a child says if it sounds silly, or if we are pressed for time, or if we do not agree with them. The temptation might be to remain firmly in the authority position of dispensing information rather than soliciting their thoughts or feelings. Yet imagine how much more you can discover about children and how much more effective you can be in guiding them along their path of growth if you take the "ask and listen" position rather than the "know and tell."

If you sense that you need to brush up on your listening skills, the following basics might help get you started:

1. **Give your child 100 percent of your attention when she speaks.** If you are preoccupied or distracted, they will know, and they will get the unconscious message "I'm not important enough to pay attention to." If you are busy or unable to give them your attention right when they need it, let them know, and be sure to "schedule" a time with them when you can give them your undivided attention.

2. **Practice showing an open mind.** When children encounter judgment, they cannot speak openly. Give them space to say what they are thinking and feeling.

3. **Hear what they have to say before you respond.** If you rush in with what you have to say before fully hearing them, you invalidate what they are trying to communicate. Don't dismiss what they say automatically (even if it seems ridiculous), and don't necessarily jump in to fix a situation before they are finished speaking. The classic example of this is the mother who runs to the principal when her child says he or she is being picked on, which of course exacerbates the situation for the child. You'll need to hear what they have to say in its entirety before you can know what they need from you.

4. **Listen between the words.** Know that if they are expressing a need or a want, there is usually a feeling behind it. If you can, try to get to the feeling. This will give you insight into what's going on and will make them feel understood. For example, if your child says

"I don't want to go to the party," recognize there is a reason and a feeling behind that statement. Asking her why she doesn't want to go invites her to express the feeling leading to the hesitation. Perhaps she feels shy, or has been getting teased by some of the kids who will be there. Trust your instincts: if you sense there is more than what they are saying on the surface, there probably is. Also, if the reaction they are having is more extreme than the situation warrants, it's a clue that there is something more going on than what they are letting on.

5. **Listen with more than your ears.** Watch your children's body language. If they aren't making eye contact, it's a clue that they are either hiding something or feel some measure of embarrassment and shame. If their body language changes or deviates from the norm, you may want to gently ask what they're not telling you. Remember to practice being nonjudgmental here!

RELAYING INFORMATION

The flip side of listening is speaking to children. When you find ways to effectively relay to them what you are trying to say, what you expect, and what you are requesting from them, you are offering them the opportunity to learn according to your wisdom and guidance. Children can't do what they don't know how to do, and can't comply with what they do not understand.

Communicating logistics is the most basic form of speaking to children. What time to be home for dinner, where to put their dirty laundry, what not to do when you have company over—all are facts that make daily life run more smoothly.

Next are your expectations. You can't assume children know what you want from them . . . without guidance, they have no idea! They can't know how you expect them to behave in a given situation unless you relay this to them in a way that makes sense to them. You will have a lifetime of instructions to convey to your child, from "don't touch the electrical socket" to "say no to drugs." Though the situations will vary from one life stage to the next, the challenge of getting your point across to your child will remain the same.

There are many good books, videos, tapes, and classes on how to communicate to your child. Here are some basics I've found highly effective in consulting with families as well as raising my own child:

1. **Speak their language.** If you put things in their frame of reference, it will help them understand what you are saying. For example, rather than discuss responsibility as a complex subject with small children line up their stuffed animals and ask them what the littlest one could be counted on to do. Then go to the next one and ask the same question. Keep progressing to larger and larger animals until they get the point that the larger the stuffed animal, the more capable it is of handling responsibilities.

2. **Explain why.** "Because I said so" is among the most frustrating reasons teenagers can hear for why they must or must not do something. Refusing to explain teaches them only that your authority is arbitrary and absolute, and causes an older child to feel helpless. If you are insisting that your teenager be home by 11 P.M., explain

why (road safety, so you can go to sleep knowing she is home, etc.), rather than just setting that as an arbitrary law.

3. **Back up what you are saying with examples that have meaning to them.** If you are telling your six-year-old not to eat glue, don't just tell him it's not good for him. Explain that it will make him sick, like the time he ate too much Halloween candy. If you are teaching your preteen that drugs are bad, have her talk to someone who works in the emergency room and can give a firsthand account about the effects of drugs. This drives your point home and supports your child in getting the relevance of the topic at hand.

WHEN COMMUNICATION BREAKS DOWN

There will be times—probably many of them—when communication between you and your child will break down. In those moments, if you cannot reestablish the link, it helps to have an outside support system you both can turn to.

Hillary Clinton wrote a book titled *It Takes a Village* [to raise a child]. These words are true in my experience. Children cannot always hear what you want to tell them. At times, they turn off and tune out any words that come from your mouth. That is one reason why you need to have a network of extended family—uncles, aunts, grandparents, friends, godparents—as part of your lives. Your extended family can reach out to your child when he or she has shut you out. A network like this shows children that the world makes a variety of resources available to them, not just Mom, Dad, and the nuclear family.

Ashley had been taking D.A.R.E., an anti-drug course, in school. She started out enthusiastic, but after a while she seemed bored. Her mom asked what had changed and Ashley said, "These situations aren't real. It's all playacting." Her mom reassured her but to no avail. Then her mother had an idea. Jim, a friend of the family, was a recovering alcoholic and had experimented with drugs in his youth. She called him on the phone and asked him if he would be willing to share his firsthand experience with Ashley. Jim agreed to take Ashley to lunch. At lunch, he asked about her D.A.R.E. course. She told him what it was like, and how she had lost interest. After she had finished, he said, "Did you know that I have had experiences with drugs and alcohol?" She looked at him wide-eyed and said, "No!" He asked her if she wanted to know what it had been like for him. She was all ears.

At that moment, Jim told Ashley exactly what she needed to hear to make the course come alive and become relevant and meaningful. He told her about that really difficult period in his life and said he would be there for her if she ever had any questions. He also said, "If there is anything I can do to help you stay away from drugs and alcohol, I will do it. Life is challenging enough without the added struggle and pain that comes with those substances." Ashley never forgot that lunch with Jim. She also never indulged in drugs or alcohol. She couldn't hear those words from her mother, but she truly heard them when they came from Jim. Consider directing your children toward one of your friends so that they can hear another point of view.

Support Is Love

All that I am, or hope to be, I owe to my angel mother.

ABRAHAM LINCOLN

Support is the act of holding someone or something up. As your child's mother, you play one of the key supporting roles in his life. You are the one who encourages and cheers him on, and who comforts him in the moments when life does not go as he might have wished. You are the invisible net beneath him that allows him to soar to great heights and catches him when he falls.

ENCOURAGING YOUR CHILD

If you want your children to reach for the stars, you need to find ways to uplift and encourage them. They will look to you for cues about what they are capable of, how high they should aspire, and whether they should forge ahead. You are your child's "life coach" who can spur her into action and show her that she can succeed.

Sue Ann's son Phillip wanted to try out for the school soccer team, but he was too nervous to sign up for tryouts. Every day Sue Ann watched Phillip in the backyard kicking his soccer ball around, and her heart ached for him. She knew how it felt to want something but be afraid of going after it, but she also knew that she wanted Phillip to have confidence in himself, so she hatched a plan.

Sue Ann talked to Phillip to try to discover the real fear behind his hesitation. He said he was nervous that the other kids would laugh at him if he missed a goal or didn't play well during the tryouts. This gave Sue Ann an idea. The next day after school, Sue Ann picked Phillip up after school and drove to a field about fifteen minutes away from where they lived. When Phillip asked where they were going, she just smiled and said, "You'll see."

Sue Ann took Phillip to a soccer practice that was going on at a school where Phillip didn't know anyone. They watched for a little while and saw lots of kids missing goals and not playing so well; one even tripped over his own feet and landed on his backside in the grass. The other kids laughed, but so did Phillip, along with the kid who fell down. Sue Ann pointed out to her son that no one at this school was laughing at anyone with cruelty, that it seemed okay to not necessarily play perfectly, and that none of them were any better than he was at the sport. Phillip was convinced and signed up the next day to try out for the team. He did just fine in the tryouts and made the team. With his mother's creative encouragement, he got past his fear and felt good about himself and his athletic ability.

Encouragement means coaxing them to try something new, as in Phillip's case, or not giving up on something they are already doing. A lot of kids are afraid to try new things. When you know it is in their best interest to try something they haven't done before, like riding a bike, it helps to do two things: minimize the risk for them, and maximize the outcome.

Minimizing the risk means finding out what is holding them back, and doing what you can to make that fear factor less threatening. Bringing the fear to light can make things seem less scary to them, and you can come up with solutions together to work through or around the fear. Are they afraid they will be rejected? That they will look uncool? That they will fail, hurt themselves, or have to change something that they don't want to change? All these are hidden reasons why kids can sometimes withdraw or refuse to venture forward and try new things.

Maximizing the outcome means showing them what they stand to gain from taking a risk. Maybe it means they can now do something with their friends that everyone else is already doing, or that they get to play a sport or an instrument they have been longing to play, or that they get to go to cool places. Pointing out and reinforcing the rewards of taking a risk shows them what they stand to gain.

Let's take the example of a child who is fearful of riding a bicycle. If he seems shy or scared, you could first talk to him to find out exactly what the fear is. Perhaps it is the idea of falling over and hurting himself that scares him or going too fast. Once you know that, you could take a trip together to the sporting goods store and get him the helmet and elbow pads that would make him feel more confident and comfortable. This minimizes the risk factor.

Next comes maximizing the rewards. Riding a bike means having the freedom to get places on his own—something most kids relish. By pointing out that he can ride to his friends' houses, you tip the balance in favor of the new activity, because he sees how it directly benefits him to try it.

Sometimes encouragement is needed when children are about to give up on something they are already doing, like playing a team sport or staying on top of their studies. Kids lose interest because they either feel diminished, incapable, or bored. When you help them find out what that wall is, together you can see if it is surmountable. You can work with them to find the impasse and develop ways through it. If you reward them with praise and reinforcement, they are far more likely to want to continue the activity. More often than not, you can motivate kids by staying involved in their progress and providing positive reinforcement for enthusiasm and achievement.

COMFORTING YOUR CHILD

Life doesn't always go the way we want it to. As adults, this is a fact most of us are all too painfully aware of. However, we've had enough experience to know that life's disappointments are not the end of the world; that we can go on, take another road, heal, and hopefully learn from them. Children, however, may not know or understand this, and their hurts and setbacks need to be treated with special care.

When children experience a setback—not getting the grade they expected, not being chosen for a team, or having their young hearts broken—your first instinct may be the universal maternal one: to kiss the hurt away and make it all better. That's one of your functions as the mom, to be the one to take away their pain and set the world right again. Sometimes this works, but when the boo-boos are bigger than just skinned knees, knowing how to comfort them is a taller order.

When Veronica's 14-year-old daughter, Missy, experienced her first romantic breakup, Missy was devastated. She spent days locked in her room crying, refusing to come out or even eat. Veronica's heart was breaking for her daughter, and if she could have taken away Missy's pain and heaped it on herself, she would have.

I've heard countless variations on this story and of course experienced times like this myself as a mother. When Jennifer didn't make the volleyball team in high school—something she desperately wanted—I felt her pain in seeing the loss of her dream. She looked as if someone had died, shuffling about the house aimlessly while all her close friends were at practice.

When things don't go their way, you can offer comfort in ways that are both soothing and helpful. It helps to keep the following four steps in mind in those instances:

1. Listen to the whole story about what was unfair, or how they were mistreated. It's beneficial for them to vent their frustration and disappointment to an audience with open ears. Try to refrain from interrupting or rushing to a solution before they have had a chance to express all their feelings.

2. Show compassion and empathy for their disappointment. This means not telling them why they shouldn't be upset! It might be tempting to list for them all the reasons why they should not let the setback "get them down," but that only serves to invalidate their feelings. If it helps, imagine yourself in their shoes, or recall a situation of your own in which things did not go as you might have liked.

3. Create a solution and a game plan together regarding what they can do about the situation. Is it time to fight for what they want, or learn a lesson from what happened and go on from there? Tackling the problem systematically (*after* they have gotten their feelings out and been heard and understood by you) gives them their power back in any given situation and gets them back in the game.

4. Respect their ways of dealing with the disappointment. Children may have very different ways of coping with losses and defeats. Respect their choices and don't force them to react as you would.

For example, what might Veronica have done for her daughter Missy after her boyfriend broke up with her? First, she could encourage Missy to talk about the situation, to express how disappointed she was, how angry she was at her ex-boyfriend for betraying her, how scared she was that no other boy at school would ever ask her out again. She would listen to the whole story, without interrupting and without offering anything other than a sympathetic ear and an available shoulder to cry on.

Next, she might tap into her compassion for Missy's situation and let her daughter know she understood how she felt. Perhaps she would think back to her own experience of shattered young love, or to a more recent disappointment that she felt was on par with Missy's breakup. She could let her daughter know she understood and assure her that all her feelings were normal and valid given the situation.

Once Missy was calmer, she could suggest a possible game plan of ways to proceed from there. If contacting the ex-boyfriend made sense, they could figure out together what Missy could say. If it was better to simply go on nursing her broken heart and get over him, they could make some plans that would put her on an active "heartbreak healing" program. Ultimately, they could talk about the life lessons available from the experience, so Missy could use the unfortunate situation as an opportunity for growth. Lastly, if Missy wanted to write a lengthy letter to him outlining her feelings, it might help to get it out on paper. Later she could decide if she was going to send it, burn it, or save it in a drawer.

You can't always take the sting away when children are hurt, but often you can help them heal a little faster. All it takes is a willingness to be there for them in their times of need, and an open and compassionate heart.

Discipline Is Love

Some are kissing mothers and some are scolding mothers, but it is love just the same, and most mothers kiss and scold together. PEARL S. BUCK

You are the one who draws the line. You determine what are acceptable and unacceptable behaviors. You are the one who reinforces their attitudes, manners, and interactions, and who provides parameters. That is all part of the job. It's your child's inherent mission to experiment, to push the envelope, to test, and to challenge. It's up to you to determine when and where to say "yes" and "no," and when to invoke consequences. This is often referred to as discipline.

Discipline has many different connotations, from training in self-control, to education, and finally punishment. The dictionary defines discipline as "training of the mental, moral, and physical powers by instruction, control and exercise." Disciplining your child can be one of the most difficult tasks you will have as a mother. It's hard to look into those precious little eyes and say "no," or even worse, to use consequences to demonstrate that their behavior is unacceptable.

Discipline is something parents must learn to apply based on their own values and circumstance, using whatever methods are most appropriate for them. It can be one of the most trying parts of mothering, yet at times it is also one of the most necessary. Your children look to you to learn how to be in the world, and it is through establishing guidelines and enforcing them that you convey that information to them. You put your money where your mouth is, so to speak, and I would bet there are very few mothers out there who relish this part of the job. Yet we do it, because sometimes the love our child needs requires a firmer hand.

SETTING LIMITS

Setting limits may not be mentioned in a pastel-toned Hallmark card, but it is part of the motherhood mix in raising healthy, happy, and socially responsible children. After all, if they don't learn boundaries from you, they will have to learn them from some other authority figure who may not be so understanding.

Saying "no" may not seem to fit the Kodak picture of Mom, but it is one of the most important words in a mother's vocabulary when it comes to safety, security, and support. No one likes to hear "no" in answer to their requests. It is the sound of rejection, of a door closing—and the reality that they can't have what they want.

Saying "no" can be difficult, no doubt about it. You may feel like you are depriving your child (especially when she is howling at the top of her lungs), or that you are a monster of the worst kind. Saying "no" can run counter to a mother's instinct to give to her child, and this conflict is certainly a test of your will.

There are four types of mothers: the ones who never say "no," the ones who always say "no," the ones who say "no" and can be wheedled into "yes," and those who say both "no" and "yes" and are firm and clear in their convictions. The test is whether you weaken and give in after sulking, tantrums, accusations, and insults.

As a mother, you can see the big picture and the long-range plan in a way that your child can't. You know that endless handfuls of candy will harm her teeth later on, while all she can see is that Mom is saying she can't have something that tastes good right now. You know children need to learn how to share as part of their growth, yet all they see is their toy being played with by another kid instead of them. When you "deprive" them of what they want in those moments, you probably won't be very popular with them for a little while. You may even hear the well-worn "I hate you!"—something no mother loves hearing. Yet your task is to do the right thing even if you are temporarily disliked for it.

Sometimes it is really difficult to know what to do. You may go back and forth, weighing the pros and cons. On the one hand you want to be the benevolent, all-giving, generous, kind, and indulgent mom. And on the other hand you want to teach your child values and set a precedent for future situations.

Knowing when to say "yes" and when to say "no" requires some skills. You say "no" when you sincerely believe that your child may be at risk or in danger. You say "no" when children ask to do something that is inappropriate for their age or any age. You say "no" to reinforce values and to set necessary limits. Your judgment on whether you say "yes" or "no" should be based on wanting what is best for your child, not wanting to avoid conflict, wanting them to like you or think you're cool.

You say "yes" when you want to empower children, Encouraging them to grow, to try new behaviors, to learn new skills. You say "yes" to reinforce taking reasonable risks, to give them some free rein, to enable them to spread their wings and trust themselves to take flight on their own. Be careful that you don't say "no" arbitrarily, to show you are the boss or to control your child. There will always be parents who are stricter and those who are more lenient than you.

When to say "no" and "yes" is an individual judgment call. No two children are exactly alike and no two parents are alike, which complicates matters. What might be a "yes" for one child could be a definite "no" for another. Therefore, it is very important to be inner-directed in your decision-making as a mother. If you hear the words "Everybody is doing it"—a phrase straight out of the children's handbook—do not give in because they make you feel like the strictest parent. "Everyone else is doing something" is not sufficient reason for you to say "yes."

Many parents struggle with the issue of allowance. They wonder what message they are sending to their child. They want the child to respect and value money, yet they want to steer clear of the entitlement mentality. If you are wrestling with this issue, you might have a conversation in your mind that sounds like this:

"If I gave Katie an extra three dollars for her allowance, what would it matter?"

"Yeah, but aren't you sending the message that whatever she wants, she can have?"

"But it's only three dollars. We can certainly afford it."

"That's not the point. You are sending a message that the more she wants, the more she gets. She gets the message that if she is persistent and wears you down over time, you are likely to give in to her demands."

"But if all her friends are getting three dollars more, I look like a cheapskate."

"Do you want her to be continually throwing more lenient parents in your face? Do you want to base your decisions on what 'everyone else' is doing?"

"Maybe I'm stuck in another era. Maybe I'm the one who is out of step with the times. What if she is being treated unfairly because her mom's ideas are somewhere in the last millennium?"

"You know that she will just keep upping the ante. If you say 'Yes' now you will have this same discussion in another three months. There will never be an end to this. Be firm. Stick to your guns!"

"I feel like a bad parent. She acts like she is impoverished. Compared to her friends, I sound like a miser. She says her social life is suffering because she can't keep up with her friends' activities financially."

"Tough! So she can't go to the movies this week. That is not the end of the world. What values do you want to communicate? She can grow up and become one of those people who can't live within her means, or she can realize that her challenge is to work with the amount of money that has been allotted to her. After all, everyone must live within some type of budget."

About this time, you have a severe headache, feel defeated, and are no closer to a resolution than you were before you started this inner negotiation. You could read books on the subject, watch morning talk shows, form a support group to see what other mothers are doing, call her friends' parents for a reality check on allowances and spending habits, but chances are you will still worry about doing the right thing.

Ultimately, your decision about what is right for you and your child can come only from your own inner truth. You must visit that place deep within you that knows what is right in each situation. Gathering information is often helpful because you have more data, but ultimately the choice about how you handle things in your family must come from you and your spouse. When you find yourself perplexed by a decision, find a quiet place and bring your journal.

Ask yourself these questions:

1. What action will support my child in the long run?
2. What message do I want to send my child?
3. Are we establishing a positive or negative pattern?
4. Will this imprint help or hinder him later on in life?
5. What decision will give my child values on which to base future decisions?

Trust the inner messages that you receive in response to these questions. You have more wisdom than you might think in those moments, and ultimately, whatever choice you make will provide valuable lessons for both you and your child.

Children will misbehave . . . that's a fact of life any mother can validate. They will disobey you, break things, say things that horrify you, do things that make you want to hide your head under the pillow. I've heard stories ranging from the horrifying to the hilarious (like the little boy who stuffed an entire bag of marshmallows into the microwave, plastic bag and all, to see if they would blow up—they did). Hopefully, yours will lean toward the latter, but you'll need to be prepared for anything and everything.

We've all witnessed the nightmare of a child screaming in the supermarket, or breaking a very expensive item in a store. In those instances, the first reaction of any mother may be frustration, or even anger. It's not the ideal textbook reaction, but it is truly human. Looking back at my experience as Jennifer's mother, I am least proud of the angry moments. Those are the times I felt I let both of us down. Even if I was justified in my anger at the time, I felt I should have been more conscious, more evolved, more controlled, and not let her get the better of me. But I'm human—mistakes, lessons, and all. What matters is not how much we flagellate ourselves for getting angry, but rather understanding how we got to that point and where to go from there.

When anger gets the best of you, it's usually because you are out of reserves and are stretched to the breaking point. In those moments, it helps to do whatever you can to diffuse your anger, to prevent yourself from doing any real damage. These are the red-flag moments—the times when some may cross the line into physical or verbal abuse. Count to ten, take a breath, go for a walk; do whatever you need to do to take the heat out of the moment. If it helps, remember that your child is inherently an innocent being who needs to be shown right from wrong, who needs your guidance. Find your compassion, if you can. At the very least, take steps to ensure that you do not lose your temper in a manner both of you will later regret.

It's normal and healthy to express displeasure when children misbehave; that's how you teach them to tell right from wrong. after that, however, you may choose to think about what you can say, without rage or blame-ridden accusations, to change the behavior if you want your child to learn more positive ways of behaving.

For our purposes here, I won't go into the many ways to discourage negative, destructive behaviors or how to reinforce positive ones. There are many excellent resources available to mothers, including books, videos, seminars, and classes, and I encourage you to seek out whichever ones resonate with you. Included in the back of this book is a listing of some of the ones I think are excellent.

If you find it extremely difficult to set limits and discipline your child, it may help to remember the following truths:

1. Teaching children right from wrong is an expression of love.

2. The limits you set for them at home will stay with them as guidelines throughout their lifetime.

3. If your children do not learn limits from you, they will be forced to learn them from other authority figures later on who may not be so understanding.

Whatever methods you choose to guide and discipline your child, know you are not alone in viewing this as a challenge. Also know, however, that everything you do is going toward the greater good of raising a wonderful child to be a fully functioning and thriving member of the world.

Getting to the root of the behavior

There is always a reason for negative behavior. Children either don't know any better, or they know better but are consciously or unconsciously choosing to disobey. If it's the former, you have a chance to teach them new behavior. If it is the latter, finding out why they made that choice can guide you toward the best way to deal with it.

Children disobey their parents for several reasons:

1. To get your attention
2. To test your limits
3. To test their limits
4. To feel their power
5. To differentiate themselves from you
6. To show that they disagree with your values, ideas, or methods

It's beneficial to take the time to determine why your child did what she did, so you can find the lessons that both of you can learn. You also may need to make some adjustments to the status quo.

Laura had a 16-year-old daughter named Zoe who, like most

teenagers, liked to push limits. When Laura and her husband went away for a long weekend, Zoe put forth an elaborate and well-thought-out argument that she was old enough and responsible enough to be left alone. Laura decided to trust Zoe and agreed, with one stipulation: no parties. She asked Zoe to look her in the eye and promise she would not have a party in their house while they were away, and her daughter did so.

No surprises here: Zoe had a party. Not a small one, either, from the looks of the house when Laura and her husband arrived home earlier than planned on Sunday morning. There were beer stains on the walls, the banister leading to the upstairs had been damaged, and the stereo speakers were blown. Laura was dumbfounded, then horrified, then furious.

Once her anger subsided, Laura sat down with Zoe to try to determine why she had so blatantly disobeyed her. She practiced "nonjudgment" as best as she could under the circumstances, and thus was able to draw Zoe out. Once the teenager saw she wasn't about to get blasted for what she'd done, she spoke more openly with her mother and admitted that she had had the party as a way to win new friends. All the other kids her age were giving parties, and she thought throwing a party would enhance her popularity.

Laura thought about what Zoe said, and thought back to her own teenage years. She remembered how hard it was to fit in, how essential it was to be "popular," and she was able to understand why Zoe had wanted to give a party. There was only one piece of the puzzle missing.

"Why didn't you just come to me and ask if you could have a party?" Laura asked.

"Yeah, right," Zoe snorted. "Like you would have said yes. You never say yes when I ask you for things."

"That's not true, Zoe," Laura responded. "I said yes when you wanted to go on the school ski trip, as long as you took my cell phone and checked in with me. I said yes when you wanted to go into the city with your friends to see the play, as long as you were home by midnight. There are lots of things I say yes to, as long as you handle yourself responsibly."

Laura's was a win-win approach for several reasons: first, she built a bridge to her daughter, rather than driving a wedge between them. Second, she showed Zoe how her perception of Laura's boundaries was inaccurate, using solid examples. Third, she got some insight into what was going on with her daughter at that time in her life, which would enable her to help her daughter find more positive ways to fit in and make friends.

If children directly disobey you and you know they know better, it's beneficial to take the time to find out why. In the long run, you'll be able to turn what could have been a disaster into a learning experience for both of you.

※

Motherhood will take many different forms, depending on the situation. At the root of every parent/child relationship—hopefully—is love, but how you express that love will vary from day to day. One day it may take the form of kisses and cuddles, the next some boundary realignment, and the next encouragement. The key to knowing what is needed when is to pay attention, and to be willing to rise to whatever the occasion calls for. Trust that you will know what to offer when . . . it's one of the innate skills with which mothers come fully equipped!

$\mathscr{T} r u t h$ #6

AS YOUR CHILD GROWS,
SO WILL YOU

*Throughout your child's life, you will be presented with
opportunities to learn new lessons.*

$\mathcal{M}$otherhood is not only about raising a child. Even though guiding and aiding in the development of a human life is the central mission of a mother, there are other dimensions to consider. The path of motherhood can contribute significantly to your personal spiritual evolution. Who you were before you became a mother will change, and you will continue to transform as you face the challenges, lessons, and rewards that every phase of your child's life will provide.

You don't cease to be a person when you become a mother. In fact, motherhood will probably provide you with some of the deepest and most astonishing opportunities for personal development. You will learn volumes about patience and tolerance, how to be assertive, when to say "no," when to give in, when to turn to a higher power, and when to simply laugh and enjoy the humor of a situation. Whatever life lessons you need to learn, you can be sure that motherhood will invite you to embrace them. Nothing evokes your internal conflicts and issues more directly and profoundly than becoming a mother!

There is no generic set of lessons that all mothers learn, since each mother is different and each child is unique. However, since motherhood is a rite of passage, the very act of giving birth to another human being brings with it some universal lessons. Each developmental stage your child passes through has its gifts, its challenges, and its lessons. You enter each stage of your child's development as a neophyte. As you learn about this new being—its needs and the brand-new world of infant and child care—you gradually shift from fear to uncertainty to competence. You consequently develop more and more self-confidence and trust in yourself. As your child continues to grow, so do you. You eventually shift from competence to mastery with each developmental stage. As soon as you achieve mastery, the cycle starts all over again with a brand new stage. My father said it well: "Parenting is tough; as soon as you figure out how to do it, they're already grown."

Parallel Growth

Being a mother, as far as I can tell, is a constantly evolving process of adapting to the needs of your child while also changing as a person in your own right. DEBORAH INSEL

The journey starts with a cell that becomes an embryo. The embryo grows into an infant. The infant grows into a child. The child grows into an adult. With each phase of human development come different sets of lessons for both of you. Perhaps your major lesson with your infant is to trust your intuition. With your toddler you may have to learn the lesson of patience. When your child goes to school, you may experience letting go for the first time. Adolescence brings boundary lessons. Young adulthood is replete with moments of tough love and unattachment. Adulthood brings acceptance, commitment, and wisdom. Every stage holds the lessons of gratitude, compassion, respect, and courage.

As you are learning your lessons, your child has his or her own to learn, embrace, and master. Your toddler may have the lesson of listening, while your kindergartner learns to share. The adolescent learns responsibility and respect, while the young adult (18–22 years) learns openness, to transcend the teen need to know all the answers. Adult children will need to learn support and causality, taking charge of their lives. Each stage automatically provides both of you with the opportunity to grow. Growing is not always easy, but your evolution as a human being depends on gradual, ongoing healthy development. If you could see your evolution from an aerial perspective, things would make more sense to you.

You and your child are on parallel growth tracks. You grow right along with your child; it's really just that simple. While your child experiences every kind of development—physical (pregnancy, breast feeding, carrying), emotional, mental, and spiritual—so do you.

Though your changes may not be as visible as your child's, you will experience an internal transformation that speeds you on your path of personal development.

Your child comes into this world clueless and helpless—two words that might also apply to you at the moment when you become a mother. What do you do? How do you hold and comfort this tiny, fragile creature? What do all those sounds mean? What are you supposed to do?

When Jennifer was born, I felt as if someone had taken a hand grenade, pulled the pin, and exploded my capacity to love. I felt limitless love for this tiny creature, so helpless, depending upon me for her every need, with the exception of breathing. I felt overwhelmed and in awe. I was also struck by the profound absence of any barrier or obstacle between us. It was as if there were a river of pure love flowing between us. I wept tears of joy, gratitude, and humility. I felt so blessed yet in a strange way undeserving of the honor and privilege that had been bestowed upon me.

Most of all, though, I felt wholly inadequate for the task of being the mother to this precious and uncomplicated being. I felt nervous that I would hold her wrong, concerned that I might make a mistake, afraid that I would somehow hurt her, or impede her development. I wanted her to have only the best, and I felt that I wasn't all I needed to be. I feared that I might not be sufficiently whole and complete, that I might not have had enough mothering myself. I was concerned that I wasn't sufficiently unselfish to do the very best for her. I had to come to terms with my feelings of inadequacy. I vowed to learn everything I could, to endeavor to do everything right, to be the best that I could be, given my perceived flaws. In the end, however, the best I could do was to grow right along with my daughter, into the mother that I am today.

Every stage of her development has taught me something about myself. I have grown to be more whole as a result of acknowledging my shortcomings. I have become more of who I am because I have been myself rather than some imitation of who I thought I was supposed to be. I have made "mistakes," many of them. It is from the mistakes, however, that I have learned my most valuable lessons. It is from the moments of insecurity, self-doubt, and fear that I have grown the most. For who grows from competence and perfection? It is only from those moments of not knowing what to do or where to turn that you grow through your creativity and connection with inner wisdom.

Every stage of life your child passes through presents new areas of growth for you. And as my father said, just when you have learned the lessons of one stage, it's immediately on to the next, where a whole new universe awaits you.

INFANCY

Between birth and age one, most children learn to crawl, pull themselves up, stand, and even walk. They make sounds and learn to say some words. They learn to use their hands and hold things. During this time, you will get to know them, and begin to feel less helpless and more confident. You will learn how to feed, burp, bathe, diaper, and dress them, how to put them to sleep, calm them when they are upset and care for them when they are sick. You will also start to identify and recognize their different sounds and cries. You will differentiate when they are scared from when they are hungry. You will learn ways to reassure them, to let them know that you are there and that they are loved. You will learn ways to help them focus, to stimulate, amuse, and pacify them. Your growth and learning will grow in direct proportion to your ability to cope with satisfying their needs. They learn daily from your guidance, and you learn what it means to be wholly responsible for another being.

THE TODDLER YEARS

Once children have started to walk, their curiosity drives them to explore their world and open anything that will yield to their strength. As they discover new sounds, they start to chatter constantly, experimenting with the tones they can utter. They start to learn at an exceedingly rapid rate. The more information you present to them, the more they can absorb. Your biggest challenge is to keep up with their insatiable desire to explore, experiment, and discover their world. Where once you couldn't wait for them to say "Mama," now at times you can't wait for them to be quiet and stop asking questions even for a few moments. As they learn to explore their world and their capabilities, you learn how to set safe boundaries for them. They learn to find their voice, and you learn how to use yours to guide them.

As soon as you think you have the two-year-old under control, a personality emerges from your little one that can totally knock you off guard with its unpredictable humor. Between ages three and five, learning accelerates once again. Learning to go to the bathroom on their own, to dress themselves, to identify people and objects, to recognize their needs and wants, to communicate with everyone they meet, and to become socialized into their larger world are all on their curriculum.

Your primary learning during this phase is to become their teacher. Realizing that they have boundless energy, an insatiable desire to learn, and the capacity to delight or drive you crazy, you will have a choice. It has been said that childhood is a natural state of mania. Children normally have lots of energy, are impulsive, and are easily distracted. You can either be their patient and supportive teacher, directing their energy in constructive outlets, or you can be their intolerant and critical teacher who constantly scolds, says "no," and is punitive in attitude, tone, and behavior. This choice will depend upon how you were parented, the degree of stress in your life, your relationship with your spouse, and how you choose to parent. You can be sure that your patience will be tested if your child doesn't learn at the rate you think is appropriate. You can also be certain that your child will delight in learning for the rest of his or her life if you make the process magical and fun; if you make it arduous and painful, your child will tune out and turn off to the learning process. This lifelong pattern in your child's relationship to learning and growing is in your hands and within your control.

THE GRADE SCHOOL YEARS
Between the ages of 5 and 10, your child will most likely be in some sort of formal education program that enables him to develop his so-

cial skills with other children. Your child will gain many things in school: mental stimulation, physical coordination, and socialization. During this time, you will have the challenge of staying connected to the development of your child, who will probably be apart from you each day for between three and eight hours. If you choose to stay connected to teachers, friends, projects, and studies, and participate whenever possible, you will need to learn about time management. You will be faced with the challenge of attending to all of the people and tasks in your life, and doing a quality job in meeting your responsibilities rather than just getting them out of the way.

THE "TWEEN" YEARS

Between 10 and 13 you will be faced with someone who exhibits a new awareness of the world around her. You may notice a new element of consumerism, with awareness of brand names, and a desire to fit in. The "tween" years are a preview of coming attractions: teenagers. This is a stage of increasing desire for independence, without the capabilities to handle it. Managing the tween years will require some supportive objectivity. Clear, firm boundaries are required from you. Don't even consider comparing these times to when you grew up. The world has changed significantly, frames of reference are radically different, and a comparison may widen the gap between you and your child. You could be perceived as a Neanderthal. The last thing a tween wants to hear is "when I was your age . . ."!

Your education during this phase involves finding a way to offer guidance while allowing your preteen breathing room. She is going through awkward changes as she begins to test her limits and yours. Chances are you will experience a similar clumsiness as a parent at this stage. It's not easy to find the right balance in dealing with tweens. However, this is your challenge and an opportunity for growth during these years.

TEENAGERS

For most mothers the years from 13 to 18 can be the most perplexing, challenging, and difficult time of all. Consider this: a caterpillar spins a cocoon in which it transforms itself into a butterfly. The entire process happens in private. One day, voilà—magic! A beautiful butterfly emerges where there once was a plain worm. Teens must transform themselves in public, with everyone commenting daily on the changes. They wake up and their feet have grown a full size overnight. Random hairs are sprouting, and the shape of their body is changing on a daily basis. Like something out of one of those werewolf or vampire movies, changes seem to be occurring in the middle of the night without their consent or control. And these are only the visible changes. Their brains double in size, their hormones and emotions rage without their approval, and a new interest in the opposite gender simply adds to the confusion.

As teens experience this metamorphosis, your learning curve involves staying centered with compassion and firmness. They embark on the white water of adolescence, while you are expected to stay grounded. You must be the ballast in the midst of their stormy transmutation. For everyone involved in it, this process is destined to be confusing. If you can stay one step ahead of the mayhem, it helps. You are the anchor, stability, and grounding, for them. If they lash out, it will most probably be at you, because you can handle it and you will still love them regardless. Part of your challenge during these teen years in particular is to resist taking anything that may be said to you or about you personally. Don't believe their outbursts. They are merely venting in the only way they know how, on someone with whom they feel safe, whom they believe will love them even at their worst.

ADULTHOOD

Then, almost overnight, before you know it, your children are grown, out of the house and on their own. Paradoxically, you experience both relief and loss. Your growth at this time comes from letting go—trusting that they have everything they need to get everything they want, and that you did the best you could. You learn how to let go, and move into the next phase of your own life.

Certainly your children will grow by leaps and bounds as they progress from infant to adult. One thing mothers never expect yet agree on is the fact that you too will grow and change. The woman you were on the day your child was born will hardly be recognizable to the woman you are the day you realize they are old enough to vote. You will be infinitely stronger and wiser for the experience of having raised a child.

Parallel growth is what nature intended for the mother-child relationship. Once you know how to care for the "easy" child, then you are given yet a greater challenge with your next one, who is a "high need" child, and so on. You will only be presented with challenges that you can somehow handle, even though at times it may not seem that way. The tests require that you transcend any barriers of insecurity or fear and emerge into a being who is blossoming into all that you are capable of becoming.

Motherhood Is About Learning Lessons

We learn the rope of life by untying its knots.   JEAN TOOMER

In the great school of life, motherhood is the advanced degree program. Everything that happens along the way is an opportunity for you to learn valuable life lessons. You can be certain that motherhood will confront you with whatever lesson you need to learn at any given time.

To prepare for motherhood, you can attend parenting classes, which I recommend, or you can read books, of which there are many. The specific lessons that I am referring to here, however, are not about how to put on a diaper, whether to breast feed, or when to potty train your child. The lessons I am referring to are the ones that come from the great school in the sky, and give you exactly what you need to learn, at just the right time.

- If you have been self-involved, you will need to learn about putting someone else's needs before your own.
- If you have resisted authority, you may have a child who will have difficulty with authority as well, only now you will be the authority figure.
- If you have become rigid, flexibility will be your lesson.
- If you are judgmental, your child will test the limits of your compassion.
- If you are powerful, your lesson will be surrender.
- If you have had financial issues in your life, a child who needs and wants more than your budget will permit might magnify them.
- If you have had issues with accountability, then you will be called upon to finally be accountable with your child; you will also have the challenging task of teaching your child responsibility.
- If multitasking has challenged you, you may have twins or multiple births.
- If you have had difficulty trusting your decisions and sticking to them, then you will most likely have this issue magnified in relation to your child.
- If you have been a dilettante, you will be challenged to be serious about shaping the life of a child.
- If you have been inconsistent in your beliefs or behaviors, you may be challenged regarding your values or integrity.

For instance, if you refused to attend religious services with your family, will you mandate that your child attend church or temple?

- If you were rebellious and broke your parent's rules, you will be confronted with enforcing rules with your child. You may need to enforce rules that you yourself broke. If you were a child who pushed the envelope, who liked to experiment, who even broke certain rules, then your past behavior will surface while providing guidelines for your child. In fact, your ethics will duel with hypocrisy. For instance, if you had premarital sex, will you be permissive or strict regarding your child's sexual activity?

The task before you is to achieve mastery over those problems that you are struggling with yourself. If you believe that you only get what you can handle, then each mother receives the perfect child for her individual growth.

Jeannie and Darlene were friends. They were both mothers; however, their experiences were totally different. Where Darlene had always struggled with finances, Jeannie was always surrounded by abundance. Darlene worried about living within her means, sticking to a budget, and making ends meet. Jeannie always seemed to have out-of-the-blue miraculous things happen when it came to money. Darlene had a child who was always asking for things, a paragon of consumerism. No matter what Darlene gave her daughter, it was never enough. Jeannie, on the other hand, had a child who never asked for anything. Jeannie kept asking if she could buy her new athletic shoes, clothes, a bike, or skis, and the answer was always "no, I'm cool with what I have."

When the two women would meet for coffee, they would compare notes and laugh about the extremely different children they had each received. The children were so opposite, each teaching her mother the lessons she needed to learn. Darlene needed to learn to establish firm, clear boundaries, while Jeannie needed to give her child the most precious gift of all, her attention . . . her time . . . her love, the gift of herself.

ADVANCED LESSONS

Some women are presented with what appears to be a graduate course in motherhood. In an ideal world all children would be born perfectly healthy and with all their capabilities intact. Sadly, however, that is not always the case. Mothers who have children with physical or emotional disabilities are given special and unique growth opportunities. Those mothers whose children fall prey to drugs, gangs, or violence are tested beyond anything many of us can imagine. It is these mothers who reach the upper echelons of growth as they find ways to shape the life of a child who is different, or difficult. As one mother wrote about her child:

> One of the reasons that I was having such a rough time myself, feeling on the verge of a breakdown, was because Steven was having one problem after another.
>
> About six months ago I found out that Steven's speech was delayed at least eight months and that he'd have to have

tubes inserted again in his ears. Luckily six months before we'd found out that he did not have permanent hearing damage from all of his ear infections. Then he was tested for his IQ. The worst thing happened when I was away on a business trip and my husband found out that Steven's growth was so delayed that he'd fallen off the medical charts. In addition, his bone development was behind by one to three months. The doctors started testing for diseases such as cystic fibrosis. That has been ruled out, but the doctors think he now needs growth hormones.

We took him to an endocrinologist who said that before starting something like growth hormone therapy, which can't be stopped, she would look into nutrition and allergies. So we then saw a nutritionist and had more growth hormone tests.

I started sensing the need to see an allergist and ten days ago I found out that Steven is allergic to almost everything! Milk, sugar, eggs, pork, apples, bananas, oranges, lemons, and yeast. He is growing now and he is going to be fine, but the process of diagnosing him, and the fear we experienced about our precious son were really difficult.

Elizabeth Kleinveld, mother of twins

If you are a mother who is presented with advanced lessons, you in particular will need to trust that the universe only gives to us what we can handle. You were selected to shepherd this child through the world, for better or for worse. It may take all your capabilities, yet you can know for certain that you will emerge more evolved, stronger, and wiser.

WHY BOTHER LEARNING THESE LESSONS?

Lessons are repeated until learned. I wrote about that phenomenon in my book *If Life is a Game, These are the Rules*, and time and again I find that statement to be true. What you do not learn continues to surface in your life as a mother until you finally embrace it.

Alyson was never particularly strong at asserting herself. It was a lifelong challenge for her to stand up for herself and to establish boundaries. As a child, she was meek and shy, and those qualities accompanied her into adulthood. Alyson had a daughter who was outspoken and demanding. Mary Ann made up for all the assertiveness Alyson lacked. What resulted was a dynamic in which Alyson allowed Mary Ann to get her way in almost every circumstance, often to the detriment of Mary Ann's best interests and Alyson's self-respect.

When Mary Ann was a baby, it broke Alyson's heart to say "no" to her. So Mary Ann would toddle around the house, putting anything and everything in her mouth, as toddlers are prone to do. She touched everything, and rather than saying "don't touch, please," Alyson bit her tongue. She was afraid her daughter would be upset if she deprived her of anything. Many things were broken as a result, including a rare and expensive vase that Mary Ann pulled off an end table and that narrowly missed her head.

As a teenager, Mary Ann learned to manipulate her mother. She got the keys to the car, money when she needed it, and permission to go out on school nights. The word "no" meant nothing to her, since it was never enforced. She didn't honor her curfew because she knew her mother wouldn't do anything if she broke it. She didn't worry about being disciplined by her father, since he worked incredibly long hours and was rarely home.

Each time Mary Ann pushed Alyson, there was an opportunity for Alyson to learn the lesson of assertiveness. However, since she was unwilling to address the problem, she kept sublimating her frustration and anger and giving in to her daughter.

The situation culminated one Saturday night when Mary Ann, then 16 years old, went out to a party and didn't come home. Alyson was frantic, and called everyone she could think of looking for her, including the police. When Mary Ann casually strolled in the next morning, Alyson was furious. She demanded an explanation, to which she got the standard rolled eyes and snort of annoyance from her daughter. Alyson's terror and anger were enough to propel her out of submissiveness, and she essentially read Mary Ann the riot act. She said that as long as Mary Ann was living under her roof, she would obey her parents' guidelines. If she felt something was unfair, Alyson would hear her out, but for the most part, Alyson's word was going to be law from now on. Mary Ann was so shocked by her mother's outburst that she actually looked a little scared and appeared to listen. The dynamic between the two didn't change overnight, but at least Mary Ann became willing to listen and negotiate.

Chances are you won't learn your life lessons until you are ready. It takes both willingness and commitment to advance along your spiritual path; or it could take an event that either makes you really angry or gives you the jolt you need. Either way, you can be certain that opportunity after opportunity to learn your lesson will arise, until you finally turn and face it.

FINDING THE LESSONS

We all have lessons to learn. Each mother will need to learn her own individual life lessons. However, there are a few basic and essential ones that most mothers I've known have had to learn on their path. They are:

- Patience
- Respect
- Priorities
- Flexibility
- Unattachment
- Forgiveness
- Strength

Patience is defined as showing tolerance while awaiting an outcome. If you consider yourself an impatient person, then you can be sure that patience will show up as one of your life lessons.

Mothers who need to learn patience usually are on a different timetable from their children. Most children—and certainly babies—do not operate according to a clock. They operate according to the dictates of their bodies. Conflicts arise when a mother is on Greenwich Meridian Time and her child is on kid time.

Penny was a Type A person who had a dyslexic child. Whenever Penny tried to help Jessica with homework, it was a disaster. Penny's time allotment for the task was a fraction of what it took Jessica to complete each assignment. Penny realized that she either had to learn patience or have her child's learning disability drive her crazy every time they did homework together.

The key to learning patience is to eliminate your time clock. Whenever you feel short on patience, ask yourself if you really need to be in as much of a rush as you believe you do. Where are you rushing to? The time you have with your child is short and precious, and losing patience only serves to fritter away moments that you will never get back.

Tip: Deep breathing is extremely helpful when it comes to learning patience. In moments when you feel your patience being tested, take a deep breath to center yourself. That will slow you down and will remind you that everything will happen as it should, when it should.

Respect means to hold in high regard; to honor yourself or another. Respecting children means elevating them to the same status you reserve for yourself and for other adults. It can be hard to be a kid, feeling powerless and diminutive. When you offer children respect, you demonstrate to them that they are worthy, and you teach them to respect themselves.

If respect is your lesson, you will be challenged by a child who always wants to do things differently from what you expect. You may feel tempted to squash his creative energy or enthusiasm if it interferes with your agenda.

Helga had difficulty with her son's passion. Joel loved playing the drums. He didn't want to go to school, get a job, or do military service. All Joel wanted to do was play the drums. Helga had other plans for him. They argued about it until one day Joel said, "This is what I want to do. Will you respect my choice and stop trying to make me into someone else?" Helga realized that day that her ideas for her son did not match with who he was. She decided to accept his choice, let go of her agenda for him, and respect his wishes. Their relationship changed as a result, and Joel did go on to become an accomplished drummer.

Learning respect involves shifting your view of your child from "less than" to "sufficient." If you remember to honor your child as an individual, you will master this lesson.

Priorities define that which is important to you; that which you put first above all else. In the arena of mothering, this often takes shape in terms of managing your resources, most specifically time. There are only so many hours in a day, and certain things that need to get done in order to keep your daily life running smoothly. As long as your children are dependent on you, they will need you to take care of them, and that includes ensuring that their basic financial, medical, and social needs are met.

Those who have the lesson of prioritizing to learn often have difficulty juggling all the many elements of living day to day. When you are on your own, this may be "good enough," but when you have a child, disorganization or procrastination compounds, and you may find yourself scrambling to keep up with the pace of everyday life.

Trudy always put off till tomorrow things she could have reasonably accomplished today. It was a habit that started in high school. If she didn't feel like doing something, she just wouldn't do it. Rather than doing laundry every week, Trudy would wait until she had no clean underwear left in her drawer before she would do laundry. Instead of buying groceries every few days, she would creatively use every can in the cupboard and every container in the freezer before finally giving in and going to the store. Bills piled up, and late notices arrived; when threatened with disconnection or eviction, she would pay the bill and the late fees. It had become a habit.

When Trudy's baby arrived she was in for a shock. At three o'clock in the morning, it didn't matter whether she wanted to get up or not, her baby needed to be fed. When her baby cried because he needed a diaper change, it didn't matter whether she was in the mood to change the diaper. When she was ready to take her baby to see his grandmother and he spit up all over both of them, she would have to stay home and do the laundry if there weren't any clean clothes available to change into. If she didn't notice the due dates on her bills, she was putting her baby's security at risk by letting them pile up.

Trudy never thought about her behavior pattern before her baby was born, and how it might impact being a mother. She never imagined that life would magnify these seemingly little things into much bigger issues after childbirth. She never dreamed that her habit of putting things off until she was in the mood, or of managing her life haphazardly would come back to haunt her once she was taking care of two people instead of just one.

Trudy's lesson was to prioritize that which needed to get done, and to do it. If priorities are your lesson, you will need to assess what needs to be reorganized and find better systems to run your and your baby's lives.

Balance is defined as living in equilibrium and finding harmony in all your roles, responsibilities, and relationships. I'll talk about this in more detail in chapter 8, but for now, let's look at it as one of the most basic lessons many mothers are called upon to learn.

Jocelyn was usually overwhelmed and overloaded. She was a single parent with a job, a hefty travel schedule, and many social commitments. Balance was her lesson because it was missing from her life. If she was to survive, she had to learn balance. Her life lacked harmony and equilibrium. She ran from one meeting to the next, always out of breath, and usually late. She started most conversations with an apology, and spent a significant amount of time searching for lost papers and miscellaneous things she had misplaced. Her two children often complained of being lonely, and needing their mother to be around much more often than she was. One of her friends suggested that she take a time management course. Her response was, "I can't find the time!" They both laughed at the absurdity of the situation, and Jocelyn resolved to consider it. That one-day course didn't change her life, but it did illuminate a possibility. For the first time, Jocelyn contemplated that her life might possibly be different. She also realized that if this were to happen, she would have to resolve to change some aspect of her behavior.

You'll know balance is your lesson if your life looks anything like

Jocelyn's. If you feel pressed, rushed, pressured, harried, or over-whelmed, it may be time to pay attention to your balancing skills. I give ideas for how to do this in chapter 8.

Unattachment means the release of expectations associated with a specific outcome.

If you have unattachment on your lesson plan it means that you have a high need for control. You most likely anticipate the way you want things to turn out, make plans, and then become fixated on the outcome. When things don't go your way, you become extremely upset. If unattachment is one of your lessons, then you will need to become aware of it, make the choice to change it, and start releasing your expectations.

Stephanie had planned a home birth. She had attended all the birthing classes with her husband and they were well prepared. They had all the equipment at home and they were ready. However, what happened during the birth process went contrary to Stephanie's plan. She had complications, had to go to the hospital and have morphine to control her contractions, and came home three days later. Stephanie's attachment to her plan made her miserable about the circumstances surrounding her delivery. Her husband held her hand, looked lovingly into her eyes, and said, "Look, we have a healthy baby, a healthy mother, three days to rest in the hospital, wonderful nurses, and I can even get some rest before you come home. Let's give thanks for our blessings." As she looked into his eyes, she realized that he was right. Her lesson was learning to be unattached to specific outcomes. It wasn't wrong to have a vision of how she wanted things to turn out, but her attachment robbed her of any satisfaction. Becoming unattached was a process that she learned over time.

Unattachment may also arise if you have a child who turns out to be different from your vision of the "ideal child." If you always pictured yourself having a highly mature kid and you end up with one who gets a big laugh out of playing childish practical jokes, or if you always envisioned that your child would be laid back and they end up a bit conservative or uptight, unattachment will come up for you. You will be called upon to release your attachment to the way your child "should be" so you can embrace and accept her just as she is.

Learning unattachment means learning to trust the process of life. The universe works in strange and mysterious ways, and when you accept that everything happens for a reason, you can better embrace unattachment. Every outcome and event, if not optimal, is at least another opportunity to grow. Knowing this may allow you to become less attached to the way you think things "should be," and be more fully present to the way things are.

Forgiveness means erasing an emotional debt. If you have forgiveness as one of your lessons, you probably become hurt easily, feel things deeply, and maybe even hold a grudge. You also have high expectations of your children and when one of them lets you down, it is difficult for you to accept.

Katrina made it perfectly clear to her daughter Mia that after she turned 18 she could do what she liked to her body; at the age of 15, however, a tattoo was not an option. One day, as mother and daughter proceeded into the sauna together, Katrina noticed a tattoo on Mia's lower back. Katrina was shocked and reminded Mia of their conversations about tattoos. Mia was surprised at her mother's level of upset. Mia told her mom that she hadn't realized how much her getting a tattoo would hurt her mom. Katrina had to find it in her heart to forgive Mia for deliberately going against what they had agreed on. It didn't happen overnight, but Katrina found the inner resources to forgive Mia and erase the hurt, sadness, and disappointment.

Whenever children do something to hurt or anger you, the lesson of forgiveness arises. For minor infractions, forgiving them involves acknowledging that either they did not mean to cause you upset, or that they are, in fact, sorry for what they did. Often it's just not worth the time or energy to stay mad at them for something small. For major infractions, forgiveness is a little tougher. It requires that you go deeper and connect with your humanity, and find your compassion for your child regardless of what he or she did.

Strength means staying aligned with your personal code of conduct and setting boundaries for your children accordingly. If you have had difficulty staying firm in stressful situations throughout your lifetime, motherhood will test you on this lesson repeatedly.

Lily loved her son Jason with all her heart. She made excuses for his gambling habit, and whenever he needed a meal, she was there dutifully to cook for him. She was torn, but she kept bailing him out of trouble every time he needed money. It wasn't as if she had excess funds. She was on a limited budget and had to watch every penny, and Jason spent every cent he made gambling. Every week, Jason showed up at her door asking for help.

Finally, Jason asked for $100 to pay for his car repairs, and Lily said "no" for the first time. He was shocked and asked her why not. She said, "You are 35 years old. It's time you stood on your own two feet. Figure it out. I don't have much money and it needs to be saved for your father and me." She was shocked at what came out of her mouth, but she knew it was the right thing to do. She stopped the pattern and became strong for the first time.

Strength can also mean needing to stay upright in situations in which you might just crumble. When things get really difficult—when your child is in serious trouble, when you feel you are at your wit's end and are ready to give up—that is the time when you will need to be the strongest. You will need to call upon your inner reserve in order to hang in there. Perseverance is a major factor in being a mother, and when you are tested, remembering the lessons of courage and strength will pull you through.

Each child is unique. You may think that after having had one child you will be proficient and able to use your experience as a template with future children. Unfortunately, life doesn't exactly work that way. The lessons you learned with one child will not necessarily be totally applicable to your next one. Each child that you have will have his or her own specific lessons to teach you.

You will continue to learn as your children do, and you will grow right along with them. It is one of the personal benefits of becoming a mother: you emerge a better human being as a result of your experience.

$\mathcal{T}_{r u t h}$ #7

THERE WILL BE
HIGHS AND LOWS

Amidst the challenges, there will be precious moments that make it all worthwhile.

$\mathcal{O}$n the crazy roller coaster that is called motherhood, there will be times when you are coasting along, enjoying the feel of the wind in your face. The world feels open and full of possibilities for you and your child, and you experience emotions ranging from delight to genuine thrill. These are called "highs."

Then there will be moments that are not so rosy. There will be times when you feel defeated by your mission, discouraged by your relationship with your child, and perhaps confused as to how to proceed. You will feel challenged, frustrated, and sometimes a little depressed at the task before you. These are what are known as "lows."

It has been said that you cannot have light without darkness; you cannot taste sweetness without knowing bitterness. So it stands to reason that motherhood wouldn't be complete without the full range of experiences . . . not just the sweet and precious ones. Managing all the ups and downs is part of the process.

What Creates a "Low"?

Motherhood is not for the fainthearted. Used frogs, skinned knees, and the insults of teenage girls are not meant for the wimpy.   DANIELLE STEELE

A low is created in any moment when your experience as a mother is not optimal. Just as a low in a love relationship can come from a huge array of factors, so, too, can a low in parenting result from any number of circumstances. The one basic truism about low points is that it is usually not possible to see them coming. Like a hurricane, you just can't predict exactly when and where one is going to hit.

"Lows" are individual to each mother, yet there are a few constants. They hit when your child does not meet your expectations, when you are worried, when your child experiences a setback or acts out in negative ways, and whenever the two of you are not in harmony. When these things happen, you move to the "challenge" end of the motherhood spectrum.

UNMET EXPECTATIONS
Part of what creates a "low" is the expectation that everything is supposed to be perfect and ideal, like a Hallmark card or a commercial for long-distance service: your beautiful child is always bright, talented, giving, easygoing, obedient, happy, and loving. When the re-

ality of everyday life turns out to be either slightly or extremely different from the expectation, it creates a disappointment. If you hold an unrealistic vision in your mind of what motherhood is supposed to look and feel like, you may experience more than your fair share of lows as a result of this cycle of unrealistic expectations, a diverging reality, and ensuing disappointment.

This was the case for Joni, the 42-year-old mother of Noah. Joni had come from a long line of literary achievers: her father was a professor of Transcendental literature, and her grandmother was a prize-winning author. Throughout her life, she took part in intellectual discourse and was part of a community of well-educated scholars. She married a journalist, and naturally expected her son to continue the family's legacy.

The problem was that Noah did not excel in school. In fact, he barely passed some of his classes. Even though they sent him to a very good private school with a low teacher/student ratio, he could not keep up. He struggled taking tests, often panicking and needing to go to the nurse's office, though Joni didn't know this at the time. All she knew was that Noah's grades were poor. Since the family gene pool favored intellectual achievement, she was confused. Why wasn't Noah excelling in his studies the way she and his father had? She was disheartened by this. She felt frustrated and sometimes even got angry with Noah, assuming he just wasn't trying hard enough. Noah, meanwhile, became withdrawn, clearly ashamed of his lack of high intellect. They were both experiencing a "low."

Joni eventually got Noah tested, and discovered he was severely dyslexic. The problem was not that he was lazy; it was that he could not process written information the same way other children could. They enrolled him in a special program for dyslexic children, and soon enough, Noah's grades improved. Both Joni and Noah shifted out of their "low."

Any time there is a gap between what you expect and what you get, you may be disappointed. The solution to easing this kind of low experience contains a choice: you can either reassess your expectation, and perhaps lower it in light of the present realities, or take whatever steps you feel are appropriate to bring your child up to the standards you have set. Circumstances will dictate which one you choose. In Joni's case, it was necessary to gather more data, adjust her expectations, and set appropriate standards for Noah. In other instances, it might be better for you to reassess your expectations.

Sheila had always envisioned having a daughter who was like her: quiet, reserved, thoughtful, and a bit on the dainty side. She envisioned having tea parties with her daughter, reading *Anne of Green Gables* with her, and teaching her to crochet later in life. It was her expectation that her daughter Chelsea would be aligned with this sensibility.

From the time Chelsea was a toddler, however, she wanted nothing to do with her mother's dainty ways. She was a tomboy from the minute she could stand up, running after her brothers, playing with their trucks, and later becoming the designated kicker for the neighborhood soccer team. She stood up to the boys at the playground when they teased her, and more than once Sheila got a call from Chelsea's teacher saying she had punched one. Each time Chelsea came home with torn jeans, a dirty face, or a bloody nose, Sheila felt like a failure as a mother. How had it come to pass that she had raised such a willful, unruly child?

Try though she did, Sheila could not make Chelsea conform to her vision of what she expected her to be. She came to talk to me to figure out how she could make the situation better, and together we discussed the options. Since she had already tried to change Chelsea, to no avail, the remaining option was for her to reassess her expectations.

"How do I do that?" she asked, looking perplexed.

"It's not easy," I responded. "Your expectations probably run pretty deep. You'll need to take a step back and look objectively at who your daughter is. Once you do that, you can more accurately assess what 'standards' you think she is capable of reaching. She may never be the 'little lady' you think she can be, but she may be a different kind of girl—one who is strong, influential, who takes charge. You may have a born leader on your hands!"

Sheila went home and thought about this. A few days later, she called to tell me she'd had a breakthrough of sorts. She realized that Chelsea was, in fact, all the wonderful things I'd suggested, and that if Sheila set a standard for Chelsea to be a stronger kind of girl, then she would ace her mom's standards. By changing her expectation, and letting go of the preset "supposed to" she had in her mind, Sheila negated a low. She opened a door within herself to see her daughter in whole new, flattering light, and to connect with the daughter that she had rather than lament over the one she didn't.

To determine which course of action is right for you and your particular unmet expectations, it may help to ask yourself if you are expecting something from your child that he or she is simply not capable of in terms of personality, skills, etc. Of course, most children have infinite potential; I am not suggesting that your child is limited in any way. What I am saying is that you want to be clear on whether your expectation is realistic—if it is aligned with who your child is and what she is all about.

Making your expectations clear

One thing you can do that may help prevent misunderstandings is to be absolutely clear about your expectations. You can't become upset with your children for not pitching in with the housework if you've never told them you want them to do so. Part of the onus is on you, to relay your expectations so you give your child the chance to meet them.

Of course, you can explain your expectations to your child any way you think will get through. One method I suggest to my clients, which can become a creative project, is the following: take a piece of paper and write down the following words: "If Living with Mom Is a Game, These Are the Rules." Then jot down anything you can think of that might be important to you. Your rules might be associated with accountability, honesty, communication, or respect. Don't let yourself off the hook with an "I don't know" response. Take time to examine what you stand for. If nothing comes up, project yourself into the future and ask yourself this: "If someone asked my child at age 16, 'What are your mother's values or rules? What is really im-

If Living with Mom is a Game, These are the Rules

1. Communicate, and when in doubt overdo it (cell phone, voice mail, e-mail).

Tell me what you are planning, what you are feeling, and what you want. Let me know what you are considering before you make decisions. Tell me what is on track, what isn't getting done, what you are concerned about, and what you need to be congratulated about. If there is an issue that is urgent, use any means you can to get a hold of me. Leave handwritten notes when all else fails.

2. Tell the truth—especially when you don't want to.

I can handle the truth. I need to know about potential problems as far ahead of time as possible. If I find out about problems down the road, or in the middle of a crisis, I will not be happy. Also avoid telling me just part of a situation and omitting key information. Keep me in the loop. Collaborate with me on problem solving, I may know some information that might be helpful.

3. Be direct and clear.

Address the topic, and present your proposed solution. Do not ramble. Do not tell me stories. Know what you want as an outcome and use your time wisely. I am delighted to give you time, energy, attention, love, and money, but please avoid deception and manipulation. Never assume anything! Assuming will often get you into trouble. Make a list of all your questions and address them all at one time. Schedule time to get these questions answered.

4. Be organized.

If you stay "on top of" all your homework, chores, and projects, I will be delighted. If not, I will be concerned. I value organization highly. If you continuously lose things and are disorganized, I will be displeased.

5. Attitude is everything.

Respect works. When in doubt ask yourself how you would like to be treated. No one ever complained about getting too much respect. Solicit feedback from those you respect. The way you come across may be different than you think.

6. Be a team player.

Things happen when we pull together. Whether the subjects

are meals, logistics and schedules, or vacations, we all need to do our part. Remember the Three Musketeer's motto: All for one and one for all! Teamwork shows up in your attitude, your behavior, and your willingness to pitch in and help out even if you are doing something that is not your "job."

7. Make every moment count.

All we have is the present. No one knows what will happen tomorrow. Create your "to do" lists. Make them reasonable, and stick to them unreasonably. Be accountable and do what you say you will do. Never put off until tomorrow what you can do today. Every choice and every action creates a consequence. Even a lack of choice or a lack of action creates a consequence.

8. Choose what you love to do and do it 100 percent.

Choose subjects, hobbies, and sports that you truly love. You need to be doing what you love so that you can get the support of everyone else in the family. If you have outgrown something that you used to do, tell me. I need to know what you are thinking so that I can support you in doing what you love.

9. Take responsibility for yourself.

Never blame other people or circumstances outside yourself. Make "the buck stops here" your attitude. You need to be "in charge" of making your life happy. Look at "stuck" areas and propose solutions.

10. Maintain an attitude of gratitude.

I am generous and appreciative. If you look at the opportunity to be part of this family as a gift and you make every day count, you will be very happy. Be grateful for that opportunity, and know that you are loved, and that I will do whatever I can to help you make your dreams come true.

portant to her?' What would she say?" I have done this exercise and I have written down my answers, which may ignite some ideas for you.

After you have completed your list, read it over and see if there is anything that you forgot or would like to include. Then make your additions or alterations. We often assume that people know what we value, what we want, what we expect. When you actually check it out, frequently the other person has quite different perceptions from what you thought. Making your list is not the end of the game, but it might be the start of the conversation. Clarifying your expectations with your child is a healthy way for both of you to make sure you are on the same page.

WORRY

Worrying seems to be a cornerstone of motherhood. No matter how much we teach them, talk to them, trust them, we still worry. It's part of the job description that just comes with the territory. There is a normal degree of worrying, and then there is an excessive level that can create a "low" for you.

The world can be a scary place, and there will always be certain risk factors out there for your children. You may teach them good values, but there will always be temptations. You can teach them to drive safely, but there are always other drivers on the road. You may teach them about safe sex, but sexually transmitted diseases are still out there. You can obsess over these factors all you like, but after you have done all you can do, the bottom line is this: THERE IS NOTHING ELSE YOU CAN DO ABOUT THEM. Worrying about things that are outside your control does no good whatsoever. Worrying never prevented anything hurtful from happening. The only thing worrying does is take a toll on you.

When you are in worry mode, you create certain biological reactions in your body. You become tense and stressed, your breathing becomes shallower, and you may even experience tightness in your chest, an upset stomach, or a headache. Emotionally, you feel strung out and overwrought. Intellectually, you may drive yourself mad envisioning all the dreadful things that could happen to your child. All told, worrying is no picnic.

Brenda was driving herself crazy, worrying all the time about her two kids, ages 10 and 12. She sent them away to summer camp for the first time, and instead of feeling excited for them on their new adventure or relishing her time alone, all she could do was worry. She worried that the little one would be homesick; that he wouldn't eat the camp food and would get sick; that he would fall in the lake when no one was looking. She worried that the older one, who was athletic, would injure himself playing sports. She could barely sleep at night as these horrible visions danced across her closed eyelids. Finally, she came to me out of sheer exhaustion.

As Brenda relayed her "worry list" to me, I wrote it all down. When she finished, I reviewed them and remarked, "Do you realize that there is not one single thing on this list that is within your immediate control?"

"Yes!" she exclaimed. "That's the problem!"

I went on to explain to Brenda that there would always be factors in life over which she had no control. She acknowledged that she had done all she could (and then some) to teach her children how to be safe, and beyond that, she needed to let go and trust both them and the process of life. Remaining tense about it had no effect other than to destroy her summer and keep her trapped in a "low." Her only option, really, was either to consciously make the choice to move out of worry mode by releasing her fears, or to stay right where she was.

The opposite of worry is trust. When you trust life, worry vanishes like smoke. When you accept that life will happen whether you worry about it or not, and that everything that happens does so to teach us something, you can perhaps let go a little and give yourself room to breathe.

By the way, worrying excessively can also have a negative impact on your children. It can make them fearful, or apprehensive. They can pick up on your nervousness and internalize it, and start to doubt their own abilities. They can wonder if they are strong enough, smart enough, or trustworthy enough. Of course, a little worrying they will expect . . . that's part of what moms do, after all.

You are probably always going to worry. As mothers, we worry when they go off to kindergarten, when they go off to college, when they have their own children. I'd bet even the President's mother worried that he might have caught a chill during his inauguration speech!

WHEN YOUR CHILD ACTS OUT

When I asked a group of mothers to describe some of their low points, many immediately told me stories about their children behaving in ways that were embarrassing and shameful. There were stories about failed classes, schoolyard brawls, lying, stealing, drug and alcohol use, and teen pregnancy. Some of the stories were extremely disturbing. One mother told me about the period when her son became involved in a gang; another told me about her daughter, who got involved with drugs at the age of 13.

As mothers, we all have issues to deal with. If your children do act out negatively, hopefully it will be in small ways that do not cause much harm to themselves or to others. Regardless of what your child does that you are not proud of, it will create a "low."

Abby had a son she couldn't control. As a young child, he was hyperactive and would wreak havoc around the house. Lamps were broken, juice was spilled, toys were smashed. Later, he repeatedly was labeled a troublemaker in school, and his behavior continued to escalate. He was suspended his sophomore year of high school for setting off a false fire alarm.

As the years went by, Abby grew more and more frustrated. She tried talking to her son, but whenever she asked why he did something, he just shrugged or he grinned and said, " 'cause it was fun." She yelled, grounded him, took away his driving privileges, but nothing worked. Finally, she took him to a psychologist, who was able to make some progress with him, though the behavior never really calmed down until her son matured.

When children act out, they are usually trying to tell you something. Their anger or frustration can come across as arbitrary, but it is almost always linked to a deeper longing or fear buried within them. If your child behaves in ways that are destructive, unethical, or even illegal, extreme measures may be required. Never be afraid to seek out professional help if you think your child needs it. There are many wonderful people and places out there who might be able to get him or her back on track, and help them work through whatever is causing the behavior.

As for you in these circumstances, it's really a matter of holding on and doing the best you can as each situation arises. You just get more than your fair share of low points on the roller coaster, though for certain you will emerge with many lessons learned. When your child behaves in any way you are not proud of, it's also important for you to remember that it's not necessarily your fault, nor a reflection of how good a mother you are.

The "Highs"

Amidst the challenges and frustrations are precious moments that make it all worth while. When your child runs into the house brandishing the first-place spelling bee ribbon, or chooses a mate who loves her the way she deserves, when she puts her arms around you and just says "I love you"—those are the moments when you remember why you embarked on this journey in the first place. Those are the "highs." These are sweet as honey and precious as gold.

When you look back over your child's young life, it will hopefully be the high points that stand out in your mind. Time has a way of erasing the bad memories and causing the good ones to take on a warm hue in your mind. One woman in my seminar, who is now in her seventies and raised five kids, put it this way:

Oh, sure, there was all kinds of stuff . . . braces, trips to the emergency room, broken bones—we had it all. The principal at our high school knew me by my first name, if that gives you any indication of how often I was called down there! But now that they're all grown and gone, a funny thing has happened: I can barely remember any of that.

What I remember are the Saturday nights we used to bundle them in the car in their pajamas and take them to the drive-in movies, the time Mike and Jack were both on the football team that went to the state championship, Susie's prom, the day Ricky got his first job—stuff like that. The photo album in my mind doesn't seem to keep any snapshots of the bad times, only the good ones . . . thank goodness!

I remember when I received an envelope from my 14-year-old daughter Jennifer. In the envelope was a handwritten note thanking me for all I had done for her. She said that she was sorry for the rough times, and she included a cashier's check for fifty dollars. She said, "I know it isn't much, but I just want to give back to you who have helped me on my path." I never expected my daughter to give me money, but the sentiment in the note coupled with the gesture was a high point for me. I still keep that note in a frame over my desk and look at it whenever I need a little boost. A "high" happens when children exceed your expectations, when they experience a personal triumph or joy, or when they express their love or affection toward you. As with the lows, they come and go, so it's key to seize and relish them when you can.

RECOGNIZING THE HIGHS

To really experience the highs, it's essential to stay aware so you can notice them, as well as noticing opportunities to create them. Be fully present so you can enjoy those precious moments when they show up. Taking your child to the playground on a Saturday can be a chore, or it can be an opportunity to have an amazing adventure on the swings. A graduation can be merely a rite of passage, or a cause for celebration. A hug can be a greeting, or a chance to connect on an intimate level with your child.

The high points come in one of two forms: as gifts, or as opportunities. The gifts appear almost magically, or as a well-earned reward. They can be good grades or a fruitful trip to buy new athletic shoes, a lovely Mother's Day card, a starring role in a school play, or an acceptance into the college of their choice. A gift is any "high" that is undeniable, and that comes directly *to* you.

The other kind of high point comes from opportunities you create. These occur when you see a window open to the possibility of something wonderful, like a lazy Sunday that turns into a picnic with your child, a moment when you pause to tell him how proud you are of something he did, or make a connection with his essence. They come *from* you, instead of *to* you.

For example, Jackie's daughter Stacey was away at college her freshman year. Mother and daughter had always been close, and Jackie missed her very much. They usually spoke every Sunday. However, it was a Tuesday afternoon, and Jackie wanted to check in and see how Stacey was doing. She called, and Stacey was thrilled at the surprise. She was in between classes and had a quiet moment to talk without interruption. Jackie was delighted because she was home alone the entire afternoon and could really talk. Their Sunday calls always involved Stacey's dad, so this was really the first time they could have a woman-to-woman chat. They stayed on the phone for forty-five minutes, and for the first time they could really talk about what

Stacey was feeling, thinking, and experiencing at this transitional time in her life. At the end of the conversation, Stacey said, "Mom, I really love you. Thanks so much for calling. It made my day." Stacey's comment, in turn, made Jackie's day as well. Jackie was delighted that she had created a precious moment where before there were miles of separation and an unused phone line.

In almost every moment, there lies an opportunity to create a high, because there is always the chance to make a connection. Keep your eyes open and you will soon be able to notice when you are given a chance to make an ordinary moment into an extraordinary one.

ENJOYING EACH OTHER'S COMPANY

Rachel was shopping for a dress for her son's wedding. She had elegant, sophisticated taste and was looking for a simple lavender gown. She was given the name of a boutique in a nearby town and asked her daughter Lili to go with her. When they arrived at the store, they realized it was not at all what they had expected. It was filled with inappropriate clothes, laden with spangles and sequins. They left the store and went for coffee. They joked about how Rachel would look covered in sequins and laughed at the thought. Rachel's taste was very simple, and not the least bit flashy. After a good laugh, they started to talk about the wedding, the changes in their family, and how they both felt about the upcoming addition to their family. They were both especially pleased with the son's choice of a bride, and with her family as well. They hadn't found time to talk in the longest time, and even though they hadn't achieved their objective, the lavender dress, it had been a special moment between them. They ended up spending the afternoon creating a "high" by simply enjoying each other's company.

Laughter is one of the strongest bonding agents. When you can laugh with your child, you get on the same wavelength. High points can happen when you have fun together. They happen when you spend the day together, doing something you both enjoy. They happen when you talk openly and have interesting conversations. They happen when you make a conscious effort to enjoy each other's company.

Elsa and her son Gerry had been going through a rough time. Elsa had grounded Gerry when she found a joint in his jean jacket, and he was angry she had gone through his clothes. It was Saturday night, and Gerry had to stay home rather than going out with his friends, so he was up in his room feeling sorry for himself. Elsa was downstairs flipping through the television channels when she came across *Tommy Boy,* one of her son's favorite movies. She went upstairs and suggested to Gerry that he come down and watch it while she read her book.

The first hour of the movie was spent in stony silence, with Elsa quietly reading her book. But as Gerry laughed at the movie, he started to loosen up. Elsa saw an opportunity to reconnect with him, so she put down her book and tuned in to the movie. Pretty soon she was laughing right along with him, and felt a personal high when Gerry high-fived her at a particularly funny and pivotal moment of the movie.

Enjoying your child's company doesn't always have to be about laughter. Sometimes it can be about sharing a hobby or sport, such as roller-blading, or going with them to a Star Trek convention. It can be about taking a walk on a crisp fall afternoon or going to a football game. Other times it may just be about cuddling on the couch or eating ice cream in contented silence.

When was the last time you spent time with your child, merely enjoying his or her company? If you can't remember, then it's been too long. It's never too late to start again. There is always time to create new precious moments.

EXPRESSING YOUR LOVE FOR THEM

Your children probably know that you love them. However, it's something they need to be reminded of again and again, like reminding them to take an umbrella when it's raining.

Give them a hug when they least expect it. Call and tell them you are proud of them. Pick up a little something you see for them that you know they might like. However you can, whenever you can, show them how you feel about them, show them that they are special, tell them that you love them. The outpouring of love immediately creates an endorphin rush for both of you, and treats both of you to an instant "high."

One day is sunny, the next may be stormy. One year is a breeze, the next is formidable. In the game of life, you rarely know what cards you are going to draw, and in the case of motherhood, you never know what is coming next. The best way to ride the roller coaster through the highs and lows is to fasten your safety belt, stay aware, take a deep breath, and be prepared for whatever happens. Though you may ride through some dark passages, there is always another bright spot just around the bend that makes it all worthwhile.

$\mathcal{T}_{r\ u\ t\ h}$ #8

REMEMBERING TO CARE
FOR YOURSELF
IS ESSENTIAL

Taking care of yourself enables you to take better care of your child.

$\mathcal{M}$otherhood has one major paradox: you must put your child's needs first, yet if you are to be effective as a mother you must attend to your own. It can be confusing, trying to find a balance between caring for your child and meeting your own needs as an individual. This is one of the greatest challenges many mothers face, and it is one of the most important ones to meet.

For centuries, motherhood has been viewed as a full-time job unto itself, with no questions asked. For many women, even up through the 1950s, a mother's only job was raising her children and keeping house. But times have changed, and the majority of women have other dimensions in their lives in addition to wife and mother.

Those who have careers presumably find fulfillment in their work and may view their work as an expression of their creativity, a source of intellectual stimulation, or a vehicle for professional development. Those who choose to be stay-at-home moms have schedules and activities (doctor appointments, lessons, sports, parties) that require attention. All mothers have inner lives that need tending.

Yet the footsteps of previous generations of women, who defined themselves as "someone's something" ("Jim's wife," "Mary's mom") still echo in our collective minds. Many women still inherently believe that motherhood must be the ultimate sacrifice—that everything you do must be done for your child. You give your life to and for your children. Your every thought is for them, every action you take is done to make their lives a little bit better. You save every penny rather than buying something for yourself. You do whatever you can to provide education, food, time, attention, and love. While dedication is admirable and wonderful, it is also important to consider that giving to your child at the *expense* of your own fulfillment can ultimately be extremely costly.

Remembering to care for yourself is essential not only for you, but also for the sake of your child. Think about it this way: how much water can one draw from a well that is already empty? Your personal resources are limited and must be replenished if you are to continually give to your child in the manner that you would like. Asking more than is humanly possible from yourself can put you at risk, both physically and spiritually. Nobody wins in that scenario, least of all your child.

I once saw a woman waiting for a bus with her two young children. She was well dressed, though her clothes were rumpled and her hair was messy. Judging from the look on her face and her nervous energy, she was clearly frazzled and overwhelmed. Her two children were playing with a hackysack, kicking it back and forth (and not apparently doing anything wrong, as far as I could see), and she repeatedly barked, "Stop!" One asked when the bus was coming, and she yelled at him, "What do I look like, the driver?" The child cowered and visibly shrank, not uttering another word. If ever there was a woman whose inability to care for herself was affecting her children, here she was.

We've all had those days when everything our children do annoys us; when all you want to do is scream "enough!" Those are the moments when you snap, when all the lost opportunities to care for yourself create layers of stress and tension. Those times can, however, be few and far between if you learn how to prevent this build-up from occurring in the first place.

It all starts with remembering to take care of yourself.

Maintaining a Balance

Keeping this balance between our own needs and those of our children—whose needs are always evolving—is perhaps the greatest challenge of parenting. ALEXANDRA STODDARD

Being a mother isn't just about having a baby and taking care of it. There is a lot more to it, and there is a plethora of things that demand your time and attention. If it's not laundry, it's a school play. If it's not soccer practice, it's an alarming report card. Emergencies can range from overturned dinners to broken bones. The one refrain I hear over and over from mothers is "there's always something!"

Beyond that, there is the rest of life to attend to. If you are married, there is a marriage to preserve and nurture. The relationship you built will need you to be present and accounted for emotionally; it can't simply sustain itself on its own. If you work, there is a career to manage, clients to serve, calls to make, meetings to attend. Not to mention trying to maintain your friendships and your social life!

There is always something that will require your time and attention. It's no wonder that the number-one challenge women face when they have children is keeping everything in balance. Where, in the middle of all this, can you find the time to care for yourself?

Isabella was a single parent with a five-year-old daughter. She had a website design business and many clients whom she kept satisfied by regularly updating their sites. She also was in a relationship with a much older man who was quite demanding of her time. Her life was busy running from her child to her clients to her partner and then back again. It was as if she were on a track with three stops. She got up in the morning and cared for her child. Then when her child went to nursery school, she attended to her clients. At the end of the day, she retrieved her child and fed, bathed, and read to her before bed. After her child was fast asleep, the baby-sitter arrived, and she would go see her partner and spend time with him and their social commitments. After four months of this routine, she sat in my office and admitted that she was thoroughly exhausted.

"You have every right to be," I commented.

"I feel like I have been on this baseball diamond. I have gone from base to base, running all the time," she observed.

"You have been. In addition to exhausted, how do you feel?" I probed.

"Empty, depleted, and disconnected from myself," she reflected.

"Are you in the picture?" I inquired.

"No. I'm trying to make sure everyone else is taken care of, but I'm not there. I only show up in the context of my relationship to someone in my life," she observed.

"How does that feel?" I pressed.

"Like I'm not there at all. I'm missing in my own life. I'm only there to make sure everyone else is happy and satisfied. When one is taken care of, I move on to the next one, and so on. Someone always needs something. And there is never any time for me. My God, look what I've been doing!" she exclaimed.

"At least you are aware of it. Bravo! Now you can make some choices your life. Perhaps you want to put yourself back into the picture. Perhaps you want to start walking rather than running. Consider for a moment putting yourself at the very center of your life and orchestrating the activities of the people around you, rather than running bases," I proposed.

"What a concept!" she mused.

This discovery permanently changed Isabella's relationship with herself. She clearly saw the game she was playing, and she saw that she was losing. She realized that her daughter, through no fault of her own, demanded as much of Isabella as she was willing to give. Her clients gobbled up her time, and so did the man in her life. All of them seemed to be insatiable. I pointed out to her that if you have to meet insatiable demands in one area of your life, it could indicate an external problem. If they come from two places, it is an interesting coincidence. However, if they come at you from every direction, it is saying more about you than about your external reality. She glanced at me sideways as if she had been caught. She had no idea how she had built up three entities that all wanted to consume her, but, she admitted, it was rather uncanny.

Isabella found out that she didn't need to stop giving to and caring for her daughter, her partner, or her clients, but she needed to make a dramatic shift. She needed to be able to make choices with all of her relationships, to create clear boundaries and, first and foremost, put herself back into her own life. The steps look like this:

1. Determine what you want from all of the relationships, including the one with your child.
2. Clarify boundaries with yourself.
3. Communicate and negotiate those boundaries with each person.
4. Find time and space for yourself to have a life.
5. Monitor your progress on a daily basis to start with, then weekly, then monthly.

Isabella first needed some time to herself to determine what she wanted. When she was clear, she then had a meeting with the man she was seeing. In that meeting she said that she wanted to change the logistics of when, where, and how frequently they saw each other. She said that she wanted to alternate nights, with one night for her to be one-on-one with her child. The next night she would be with him at her home, and the night after that she would hire a baby-sitter and have an evening to herself, and on the weekend, they could have a night out together. She met with her baby-sitter and communicated her plan. She decided to change everything she could so that she could try out different scenarios and see what felt right to her. She also started taking singing lessons. She had always dreamed of singing, not professionally, but at least outside the shower. She knew that singing lessons would be an activity just for her, and that this was sorely needed in her life at this time. Her plan worked, and she started to feel she was at the center of her life, rather than running bases around everyone else.

Are you in balance? If not, are you ready to take the steps that will get you there?

Preservation of Self

In parenting, just like in a romantic relationship, a person who is whole and complete is better equipped to care for someone else. If you forget to care for yourself, you cannot really be helpful to anyone else. On every airplane flight attendants give the same briefing. They tell the adults to put on their own oxygen masks first, before helping their children. Why? The answer is simple: because unless you are alive and breathing, you are of no help to your child.

Caring for yourself means more than taking baths and sitting in a recliner with your feet up, candles lit, soft music playing in the background, and a glass of Chardonnay by your side. That's only one dimension of the picture, and only valid if those elements resonate for you. There is much more to caring for yourself than just relaxing, though of course that is an important part of the picture. It also means listening to your inner messages and honoring your spirit. It means knowing what rejuvenates, revitalizes, and restores your energy, and then doing those things for yourself so that you stay whole, complete, and centered.

If you need convincing about how essential caring for yourself is, here is a short list of consequences that can result if you don't:

- You'll feel exhausted and depleted.
- Your health will suffer.
- You may resent your children.
- You will become short-tempered.
- Your children will fail to learn self-preservation habits from you.
- Your marriage and other primary relationships may suffer.
- Your spark or twinkle will become dim.
- You will look harried, hassled, or frazzled.
- You will start saying "I don't know" more often when asked what you want.
- You will be resentful and jealous of others who look happy, balanced, and fulfilled.

Caring for yourself means that you put the time and effort into finding and doing things that nurture you, physically, emotionally, and spiritually. It means that you make sure your tank doesn't get so low that you are cruising on fumes, and that your connection with yourself does not get too frayed. The best mothers are the best people, and being an optimally functioning human being means giving yourself the necessary sustenance.

A woman I know sends a gift certificate for a massage to each of her friends right after they have a baby. She figures that everyone else will spend money on gifts for the baby, so she gives the mother something just for herself. She says that her friends tell her it's the best thing they received!

Of course, massages are wonderful, but sustenance goes way beyond that. It starts with the basics, which include things as simple as carving out time just to be by yourself, free from any responsibilities. This can be challenging when your child is a baby, but if you're willing to be resourceful, you can find a way. If you are not fortunate enough to have a friend or relative nearby who can take care of your baby for a few hours, or you don't have the means to hire someone, then create co-op child care with other mothers you know. Time alone is precious, and downright priceless when you are a mother. If you do nothing else for yourself, make sure you find some way to give this to yourself. It is one of the best ways to keep yourself grounded.

Holly came to see me on the advice of a friend when she started to feel depressed. She knew something was off and was hoping I could help her sort out what was going on. Holly wasn't a "bad mother"—not by any stretch of the imagination. Her children were all healthy and well-adjusted, and she and her husband were often complimented on how terrific their kids were.

Holly wasn't as present as she perhaps wanted to be, however. She often rushed through activities with her kids, as if being with them was one giant "to do." She always felt like there was something she was supposed to be doing, focusing on the next activity instead of fully engaging in the present one. She described having a sense of restlessness and unhappiness.

I asked Holly what she was doing to care for herself. She gave a big dramatic sigh as she admitted that she did not engage in anything that was not directly related to her kids. As we talked more, I learned that Holly used to love to go antiquing before she had her three children. She loved wandering around in musty old shops, searching for hidden treasures. Like so many women, though, she let her hobby fall by the wayside amidst diapers, bottles, carpooling, and parent/teacher nights.

I encouraged Holly to resurrect her old passion, and take a day to go visit some of her favorite old haunts. She asked her husband to watch the children on a Saturday afternoon and drove to a town about an hour away from her home that was well known for its antique shops. She spent the afternoon doing what she loved. As she walked through the various shops, an old part of herself that she had long since forgotten resurfaced. She had a terrific day, and despite the fact that her only purchase was a little iron lamp for twenty dollars, she felt rejuvenated.

The following week, Holly felt more present and alive with her family than she had in years. She felt centered again, and able to focus on them. She vowed to take one Saturday a month to herself from now on to do something just for herself.

Olivia's touchstone was different from Holly's, but the inner reward was similar. Olivia missed going to lunch with her friends—something they often did before they all became mothers. She called a few of them and made a plan to meet on a Sunday for lunch outdoors by the marina. They asked their husbands to watch the children and had a great time laughing and catching up on old times. That lunch has now become a tradition that gives all four of these women an emotional touchstone.

What activities make you feel good? What do you like to do that makes you feel like yourself? What are the touchstones in your life that keep you aligned with who *you* are as a person?

Perhaps nature nourishes your being; if it does, find time to be in natural settings so that you fill up your tank. If music revives your depleted reserves, then make sure that you have your favorites in your collection of CDs both in your car and at home for those moments of restoration. If yoga, cycling, hiking, or dance makes you feel connected to yourself, then find a time and place and make space for this activity. If you are less active, maybe you require time for meditation, prayer, and reflection. If art is a source of solace, then schedule time to visit galleries.

Take the time to determine or recall what nurtures you, and make a promise to yourself that you will do these activities often, if not daily. If it helps, make a standing date with yourself or with people who revive you. If your spirit is renewed on a regular basis, then you will not feel depleted, exhausted, or empty. Energy and vitality are consumed like a commodity. Energy is there and then it is gone. You must replenish it one way or another if you are to be effective. No one will watch out for the restoration of your energy. It is up to you to monitor your vitality, to know what you need to do—to what degree and how often—to recharge your batteries on a regular basis.

The Way You Treat Yourself Impacts Your Children

The influence you exert is through your own life and what you become yourself. ELEANOR ROOSEVELT

In *If Love is a Game, These are the Rules*, I wrote: "At its core, loving yourself means simply believing in your own essential worthiness. It is nurturing a healthy sense of positive self-regard and knowing in your heart that you are a valuable link in the universal chain. Loving yourself also means actively caring for every facet of yourself. It shows up in every action you take, from putting on a sweater to protect yourself from a chill or leaving a job that does not fulfill you. It means tuning in to your own wants and needs and honoring them." When you are able to believe within yourself how valuable you are, you are then capable of bestowing that gift of self-love on your child.

You are your child's role model. If your child sees you denying yourself, it will send the message, "Your mother doesn't matter." If you don't respect yourself, your children won't respect you. If you break your commitments to yourself, they will learn to do this by example. The greatest gift you can give your child is the example of a mother who is living her dreams.

Mary Pipher, Ph.D., the author of *Reviving Ophelia*, was inspired by her mother. Her mother didn't worry about the opinions of others. She knew what she wanted and she went after it, unconcerned with the approval of others. She went to medical school at a time when women didn't do that sort of thing. She received her master's degree in chemistry during the Great Depression from a state university in southern California. Throughout her life, and as she faced death, her mother confronted whatever challenges came her way. The most important thing Mary Pipher's mother taught her was to do the right thing even if it scared her. As a result, Mary was inspired to take on life's challenges with dignity and determination. She spent years doing groundbreaking research on the lives of young girls and went on to write a *New York Times* bestseller. Might she have achieved the same level of success without her mother's influence as a role model? Perhaps, but her chances were greatly increased by having a mother who showed her the value of living her dream.

Of course, at times you need to sacrifice for your children, but if you can show them the way to joy, happiness, and fulfillment through your own life, then they can get a sense of the possibilities, learn how to tackle challenges, see how to overcome obstacles, and turn their fantasies into reality. A mother is a role model. Beliefs about what is possible in life are formulated by watching a mother fulfill her own dreams. Whether you believe you can or you believe you can't, that belief system is transferred to your child. This may pertain to dreams or wishes or goals. Your child may do the same as you or the exact opposite, but you can be absolutely certain that the seeds of motivation are planted by you.

When you treat yourself with respect, kindness, caring, and integrity you demonstrate to your child the fundamental qualities of self-esteem, self-respect, and personal honor. If you forgive yourself, you show your child how to forgive. If you respect your needs, your children will respect theirs. If you listen to and honor your inner messages, your children will respect their inner radar. Your internal beliefs and expectations will be reflected in the way your children learn to treat themselves.

Ella watched her mother every day. She watched how she was raised along with her five brothers and sisters. Her mother diligently did the laundry, the cooking, the mending, and the housework. She scrounged aluminum cans from Dumpsters to earn milk money for the children. Ella watched her mother's dedication for eighteen years, and she vowed that she would make her mom proud someday. Ella wanted to make something of her life for her mom and for herself. She didn't want to live the life her mother had lived, and she also wanted to give back to her mom. Ella learned about hard work, dedication, and commitment from her mother. She learned about giving back to those who sacrificed on her behalf. She also learned that she wanted a better life for her children and for herself. Ella went to school and became an engineer. She specialized in environmental issues, and today Ella Williams is the CEO of Aegir Systems, a global firm that provides engineering and technical services to the defense, transportation, and security industries.

What lessons are you teaching your children about how to treat themselves, or what they are capable of? Look in the mirror and you'll discover the answer to this question.

Passing Along Unresolved Issues

We all have issues; that's just a fact of life. Even the most well-adjusted people I've come across have beliefs and behavior patterns that they do not consider ideal. Life will, of course, continue to present you with situations and opportunities to work through these issues. Yet there is no single event in your life that will bring your issues to the surface faster than having a child.

If you are a perfectionist who needs everything in its place, having a newborn will push every button you have, since newborns bring with them all kinds of chaos and disorder. In the beginning, there are no established sleeping or eating patterns, there may be "stuff" everywhere, and your child can and usually will spit up just at the moment when you are about to walk out the door.

If you have trouble handling money, you will find yourself stretched to the maximum by your child's medical needs, braces, tutors, wrist guards, designer jeans and athletic shoes. Children cost money, and unless you have a unlimited supply, you'll need to learn how to budget and cover costs in order to provide what is needed.

If you are someone who tends toward fits of anger, you will certainly find yourself in situations that try your patience and push you to your limit. The choice you will need to make in all of these situations is twofold: one, do I want to let this issue affect my child, and two, do I want to pass this issue on to them?

Issues get passed down from generation to generation right along with the handmade linens, china, and other family heirlooms. How often have you heard the phrase "the apple doesn't fall far from the tree"? People use this axiom because so often it is true, though the qualities and behaviors that are passed along are not always the most beneficial ones. Certainly your daughter may inherit your athletic ability or your son may possess the same knack for numbers, but either of them could just as easily pick up and carry on some of your unresolved issues that are not quite so desirable.

Studies have proven that children of abusers tend to be abusers themselves. It is all they know, and they unconsciously process this behavior as normal. Though this is an extreme example, it is the one that has been the most documented, and it proves the point that unresolved internal issues get passed from parent to child. So if you have not been motivated up until now to acknowledge your own personal issues, now might be a good time to do so.

The following are the "hot spots" with the greatest charge—the areas where the majority of people most commonly harbor issues that might negatively affect their child:

- Money concerns
- Fear of the future

- Sex
- Food (eating disorders)
- Tendency to deny the reality of unpleasant situations
- Control or perfectionism
- Suppression of emotions
- Inconsistency in moods, behaviors, attitudes
- Intolerance (hate, prejudice, etc.)

One common area in which unresolved issues get passed on is the area of sex, or more specifically, discomfort about sex, as in Dora's case. Dora grew up in a strict Catholic middle-class family. To her, her upbringing appeared pretty normal, and she never questioned her parents. She was a good girl and did what she was told. When Dora grew up, got married, and had a daughter, she raised her daughter in much the same way she had been raised. The only problem was that Dora's daughter wasn't as obedient and as well behaved as Dora had been. Her daughter, Justine, questioned everything. When Justine started asking Dora questions about sex, Dora was mute. She didn't know what to say. No one had ever talked to her about sex, and she felt unprepared to address the topic. But Justine would not stop. She kept badgering Dora with questions about where babies come from. Then she asked about sanitary napkins, breasts, the male anatomy, and every other conceivable sex-related topic. Dora was mortally embarrassed. She didn't know how to react. She didn't know what to say. She just went to her room and closed the door.

When Dora's husband asked her why she wouldn't answer Justine's questions, Dora became defensive and said, "You just don't talk about such things." Her reaction was a clue to both of them that her strict upbringing had had more of an effect on her beliefs about sex than they had imagined. Dora was passing along beliefs about sex to her daughter without ever having to say a word.

Dora's issue surrounding sex could have created a situation in which her daughter internalized the same beliefs and discomfort. Thankfully, Dora's husband intervened and encouraged Dora to seek professional help to work through her mental block against talking about sex. The situation ultimately became resolved. Justine received the information she requested through conversations with her dad, and then eventually with her mom, and books. Dora worked out her issues about discussing sex, and her husband felt as if he had helped the members of his family face an uncomfortable situation in a healthy manner rather than merely brushing it under the carpet.

Another common hot spot is fear. I mentioned earlier the impact it has on children when they see their mothers living out their dreams; the effect on children is reversed when their mother is afraid of life, as in Judy's case.

Judy was raised by an overprotective mother who worried incessantly about her and her sisters. They were always the ones wearing hats and sweaters, even on days when it was 60 degrees outside. They were the ones who had to be home by nine on weekend nights as teens, and who had to call home from college every single night to let their mother know they were okay. Judy's mother was so fearful of what might happen in any situation that she always encouraged Judy to play it safe. "Don't get your hopes up" and "Don't get carried away, dear" were two of her mother's favorite refrains. As a result, Judy grew up thinking the world was a scary place, to be navigated with caution and dread.

Judy noticed the behavior pattern surface with her own children almost right away. She worried constantly and was unable to leave her children with a relative or baby-sitter for even a few hours. Judy was fortunate, however: she noticed her own behavior pattern and was willing and eager to break the link, so that she would not pass on the legacy of fear generated by her own mother. She wanted her children to experience life as something to be seized and relished, and not cower in a corner terrified.

Perhaps there is a situation in your childhood that you accepted as normal that in reality wasn't. Maybe you need to take a closer look at your perceptions, beliefs, and behaviors and see if you want to make some changes. If you have a sense that there might be something that needs to be brought to light, ask yourself these questions:

1. When some of your beliefs from childhood are questioned, do you respond, "We've always done it that way"?
2. Are there behaviors that, when questioned, you become defensive about?
3. Are there subjects that you simply avoid because you are uncomfortable?
4. Do you feel incapable of confronting a situation that you know isn't right?
5. Are there family or religious traditions that you have never questioned?

If the answer to any of these questions is "yes," it may be helpful for you to examine that issue more closely to see whether there is a behavior pattern you want to change. I'm not suggesting that this is easy: change is one of the most difficult things to face and deal with. But if the willingness is there and you open the door to a new awareness, you can begin the process that will ultimately benefit both you and your child.

BREAKING THE LINK

In order to break the link so that you can ensure you do not pass along your unresolved issues to your child or allow them to affect the way the two of you relate, three steps are required:

1. **Become aware of your issue.** This means being willing to take an objective look at yourself and being honest about what you see. If you want, consult someone who knows you well and whom you trust. Ask them what they see from the outside to get a perspective on the things that might be holding you back from mothering your child in the most optimal way.

2. **Acknowledge what is true about the situation.** Get clear on what exactly is going on, how it is affecting your child, and how you would like things to be different.

3. **Make the choice to break the link.** This is done by becoming consciously aware of your issue and either working it out so it is no longer a problem, or choosing to not let it play out in the dynamics between you and your child.

Here is an example of how this might work:

Michelle had been what you might describe as a "control freak" her entire life. She liked things "just so," and became anxious whenever anything was out of place. She became very anxious at any sudden change of plans or any kind of disorder, and she even had panic attacks when situations went too far beyond her control. Most of the time she managed to conceal how deeply her need for order went, but anyone who got a look into her color-coded closet with its ultraneat rows of hangers or her fastidious rolltop desk caught on pretty fast.

Michelle always kept her daughter Jill extra neat and clean when she was a baby, regularly changing her diaper every two hours whether it was dirty or not. She kept Jill on a regimented sleeping and eating schedule and never varied from it. As Jill got a little older, she learned to never challenge Mommy's way of doing things; otherwise her mother would get very distraught.

When Jill was old enough to attend kindergarten, Michelle took pains to dress her immaculately every day, in outfits with matching socks and matching bows for her hair. She was very upset when Jill came home one day with her panties in a plastic bag and a note from her teacher saying she'd had an "accident." Poor Jill was mortified as her mother berated her for her lack of discipline.

One day, Jill's teacher called and asked Michelle to please come in and see her. At that meeting, Jill's teacher gently told Michelle that Jill was the only little girl in her entire class who wore a dress every day. All the other kids wore play clothes that they had chosen themselves.

"If you don't allow Jill to start making her own choices about what she wants to wear, she'll have difficulty making choices and learning to express herself later on," the teacher told her. "I know it's hard, but you have to let kids be kids." Then she laughed. "You should see some of the outfits these kids pick out for themselves! Last week one of them wore their pajama bottoms with a turtleneck sweater! But I'll tell you one thing, that kid was as proud of himself as he could possibly be."

Michelle heard the teacher's words like a shot ringing in her ears. She knew that the old issue of whether she could relax her perfectionist behavior had surfaced again. Part of her knew that the teacher was right—she needed to let Jill choose her own clothes, even if it meant going to school in pajama bottoms (a thought that made Michelle shudder). Michelle came to talk to me, and together we went through the three steps.

First, Michelle acknowledged that she had an issue with control. That part was easy—she had been told that repeatedly throughout her entire life.

Second, Michelle acknowledged the reality of the situation. While she might feel more at ease having Jill look perfect every day, her needs were getting in the way of Jill's happiness, as well as her development of self-expression and creativity. She admitted she did not want Jill to have the same issues with control as she did.

Third, Michelle chose to take strides to change the situation. While she knew it would be hard (and maybe even impossible) for her to completely change her behavior, she mapped out new ways to react when relating to Jill. For example, if Jill asked for something that varied from their routine, Michelle would recognize her feeling of panic as a sign that she needed to step outside her own way of thinking and assess Jill's request from a more objective perspective.

It was a long road, but Michelle managed to break the link and ensure that her daughter would not carry on a legacy that had caused her such distress. Jill never did wear pajamas to school, though some of her outfits stretched Michelle's new tolerance to the limit!

Do you have issues that you do not want to pass along to your child? Do any of the "hot spots" on the list ring a bell with you? If so, you'll need to work especially hard to ensure that you pass along to your child only the most positive aspects of yourself.

It is up to you to remember how essential it is to care for yourself in addition to caring for your child. The women who are wise enough to ensure that they have a rich life of their own find the experience of motherhood the most fulfilling, and their children grow up knowing how important it is to care for themselves. Maintain your sense of self, and you will be passing along the most valuable legacy a child could ever hope for.

Truth #9

THERE IS NO SUCH THING
AS A PERFECT MOTHER

The best you can do is your best.

$\mathcal{M}$ost mothers strive to be perfect. It simply goes with the territory. You want to be all that you can be and do everything right. After all, when you were growing up you probably said, "When I have a child, I'm going to . . . ," and now this is your opportunity. You are eager to do it all: raise fantastic kids, make great quiche, look terrific. You want to be patient, loving, and kind, take care of all the tasks in a twirl, and show up for every recital, ball game, and school play, on time, relaxed and poised. You want to be on top of the latest theories in child psychology, and savvy about motivating, reinforcing, rewarding, and disciplining your child using the most current and cutting-edge methods. You want to be a guide and mentor to your child, a friend and companion, and to be way cool and on top of it all. That's a pretty tall order!

Where does the desire to be the perfect mother come from? There are several places. If you had a wonderful mother, you will desire to emulate her and try to follow in her footsteps. If you had a dysfunctional home, you will want to make up for what was missing in your childhood home. You may have picked up on messages from society and the media that mothers are expected to be able to handle just about anything and everything. Or you may simply aspire to be the very best you can be.

During the last one hundred years, the image of motherhood has undergone a major evolution. In Norman Rockwell's time, the perfect mother was pictured serving a magnificent Thanksgiving turkey to her grateful and eager family. She was round, rosy, and smiling. The invention of television made it possible for one idealized image to dictate a norm, or standard. For the first time in history an entire culture shared the same visual image of mother and family. The ideal mother of the 1950s was portrayed in programs such as *Leave It to Beaver*, *The Donna Reed Show*, and *Ozzie and Harriet*. The women in those popular television shows were totally dedicated to their families. These TV mothers and role models were always cheerful, pleasant, kind, organized, patient, compassionate, and calmly on top of everything. They set the standard for the perfect mother. Their children never got into any serious trouble, and the worst thing that might have happened to disrupt their daily existence was a burnt roast or a minor incident with a slingshot.

Today, television has provided us with new role models for mothers. We have everything from the "tell it like it is" kind of mother in

Helen Hunt from *Mad About You*, to the struggling single mom Sela Ward plays on *Once and Again*, to the epitome of the psychological manipulator, Nancy Marchand on *The Sopranos*. With all the different examples of mothers in the media, it is sometimes difficult to know what to expect of yourself as a mother—to know what is fair, realistic, and attainable, or moreover, what is "acceptable." It isn't easy to find the single definition of the "perfect mother" anymore.

The basic desire to be the best mother, to provide for your children and equip them with everything they require to be happy, successful, and fulfilled in life is the one common baseline for the majority of mothers. It is, however, that desire to be the best and do what's right that produces the greatest guilt as well. Whenever you fall short of the perfection bar, you will automatically experience a degree of guilt. If you feel as if you could always have done better and your best just wasn't good enough, then you suffer from the perfect mother syndrome.

Even though we know that perfection is not attainable, we still pursue it. Why? Because every mother has a brief moment in which to shape a life. Stop for a moment and consider the magnitude of that opportunity. What if the life you influence could one day impact millions of people and possibly change the course of history? What if the person whose life is entrusted to you grows up to find the cure for cancer or a way to end world hunger, or is instrumental in ending war on the planet? They could grow up and become a Mother Teresa, a Winston Churchill, or a Gandhi. After all, all of them had mothers. All their mothers had a chance to teach them values, morals, and integrity. All their mothers used their skills, knowledge, and intuition to raise magnificent beings. Is it any wonder we feel so much pressure to get it right?

The bottom line is this: no mother is perfect. Gandhi's, Churchill's, even Albert Einstein's mother wasn't perfect. Each one made mistakes and learned as she went along. Each one most likely tried the best she could. Some days she felt as if she got it right, and other days she may have wondered why you didn't need a license to become a mother. In the end, the best you can do is your best and learn the life lessons presented to you along the way.

The Comparison Game

Falling short of perfection is a process that just never stops.

WILLIAM SHAWN

Lisa had her first baby when she was 38 years old. Though it is far more common today for women to have children later in life, she still was the only woman over 35 at Gymboree with her baby. She would often look around the room at the new mothers in their twenties and wonder if she was cheating her son in some way. Would he miss out on certain experiences by having parents who were older? Did she have the same stamina as her younger counterparts?

When you compare yourself to other mothers who are younger, who are full-time, who have more energy, who were born to be mothers, you can feel inadequate and guilty, as in Lisa's case. There will always be some mother in the playground who seems to know how to do it "better," someone in your child's class who can bake fabulous cupcakes, knit sweaters, hold down an important job, and still find time to be a Scout leader. You may look around at your friends and wonder if their style of mothering is superior to yours. Perhaps they are better endowed financially, or have more time on their hands, or seem to be magically blessed with superhuman maternal instincts. Maybe their kids seem to be better behaved, smarter, or more popular in school.

Are any of these mothers "better" than you? That's a hard question to answer, mostly because the definition of "better" is so subjective when it comes to parenting. What really matters, though, is the connection between you and your children, and how closely you are aligned with your vision of how you want to raise them. The key is to connect with the mother within you and determine what it means to be and do your best with your child. You can look around and compare yourself to others all you want, but no one ever really wins when mothers play the comparison game—least of all the children.

When you find yourself caught in the trap of comparisons, it can help to return to your vision of the kind of mother you aspire to be. When you recall your own personal definition of a "good mother," the comparisons melt away like snowflakes. You return to your inner purpose and can channel your energy into being *your* version of a good mother, instead of worrying about living up to someone else's.

In moments of comparison, you might want to complete the following statements, either in your mind or on paper. As always, I recommend writing out your responses, because there is power in seeing your words take physical form:

1. For me to be a good mom, I need to be . . .
2. For me to be a good mom, I need to do . . .
3. My realistic expectations for myself as a good mother are . . .
4. In order to satisfy myself as a mother, I must . . .

Answering these questions will help you realign with your own personal vision of the kind of mother you are striving to be. It restores your sense of purpose, so you can focus on your own path as a mom, not on the differences between you and all the other mothers out there.

Sherrie, whose children are now grown and out on their own, remembers showing up for a parent/teacher night years ago when her son was in junior high school and overhearing the teacher compliment another mother on how diligently she tutored her child in algebra. The teacher complimented the other woman on how dedicated she was to her child's learning. Sherrie felt a pang of remorse when she heard this; she never tutored her son on his algebra, as she assumed he would ask for help if he needed it. She was really getting upset with herself, berating herself for not paying more attention to her son's schoolwork, as she approached the front of the line for her one-on-one conference with the teacher. By the time she got to the teacher, she was ready to plead for the teacher's forgiveness and to swear that she would be a better mother.

"Oh, Mrs. Moore," the teacher gushed to Sherrie, "I'm so glad to finally meet the parent of one of our brightest stars. You must be so proud of Andy—he seems to be a real natural when it comes to math!" It was all Sherrie could do not to audibly breathe a sigh of relief. After that, she promised herself she would never again automatically assume someone else was a "better" mother than she.

Of course, if you see another mother employing methods or philosophies that you admire, there's absolutely nothing wrong with borrowing them to make some modifications to your own. The key is to ask yourself if you are doing so because you genuinely respect her idea and want to apply it to your mothering, or because you automatically assume that another woman knows more than you.

Simone, a 22-year-old mother of twins, learned quite a bit from observing her next-door neighbor, who was ten years older than she was and already had four kids by the time Simone gave birth to her babies. She observed her neighbor creating fun games to keep her kids busy on long, hot summer afternoons and was inspired. She often watched this woman to see what she did when her children misbehaved and adopted her system of "time outs." Simone knew this woman wasn't necessarily a "better" mother than she was—just more experienced. She emulated what she admired about this woman, gleaning valuable ideas and molding them a bit to create her own methods.

The Internal Report Card

The ideal mother, like the ideal marriage, is a fiction.

MILTON R. SAPIRSTEIN

Within every mother is an internal report card. You may be conscious or unconscious of this checklist, but this is the standard against which you measure yourself. You have exactly twenty-one years to complete the first four phases of child-rearing: infancy, childhood, adolescence, and young adulthood. During those formative years you have the opportunity to satisfactorily complete everything that is on the motherhood checklist. You will only know if you have succeeded after your mission is completed.

The list is everything that you can imagine you might want to do for and impart to your child. It is everything that you want to share, to show, to teach, and to equip your child with before they leave the nest. This checklist includes the loftiest expectations of every aspiring perfect mother. It describes the outcome—healthy, fully functional, mature, well-adjusted children. Here is the checklist:

Physical: You want to ensure that they know . . .

How to care for themselves
Basic nutrition
How their bodies work
Personal hygiene

The value of exercise and its effect on them
How to treat their bodies with respect
How to accept their bodies
How to honor their bodies
How to make choices that are in their best interest in terms
of their bodies

Mental: You want to ensure that they know . . .

How they absorb information
How to approach learning something new
How to apply themselves
How to make decisions
How to problem solve
What type of mental stimulation they require
What to do to fulfill their potential
How to deal with stress and overload

Interpersonal: You want to ensure that they know . . .

How to form different types of relationships
How to share
How to communicate
Teamwork
How to get along with others
How to negotiate
Who to choose and whom not to choose

How to understand and deal with gender differences
How to give and receive support
How to establish and manage boundaries

Emotional: You want to ensure that they know . . .

How to love themselves
How to give and receive love from others
How to preserve their self-esteem
How to receive feedback nondefensively
How to manage their emotions
How to deal with disappointments
How to be resourceful
How to rebound
How to get what they want
How to deal with defeat
How to heal a broken heart
How to identify, sort out, and process emotions

Life skills: You want to ensure that they know . . .

Who they are
What their strengths and weaknesses are
How to manage their time
How to establish priorities
How to meet deadlines
How to set a budget

How to live within their means

How to make appropriate choices

How to trust themselves

How to learn from everything that happens

How to get their needs met

How to choose a career

How to choose a partner

How to earn a living

How to maintain a healthy, positive relationship

How to maintain a positive attitude

How to be responsible for their own satisfaction in life

If your child passes all the subjects on the list, then you receive an A in motherhood. If you received an A, we could, in essence, call you the Perfect Mother. Of course, if you were the perfect mother, you would blush, and say you weren't and that you didn't deserve the title (for isn't the perfect mother supposed to be modest, as well?).

If, on the other hand, your children don't embody everything that is on the list, you can be sure there will be numerous opportunities for them to obtain those qualities down the road, from a variety of different people in their lives. If your children don't possess these qualities, you haven't *failed*, it just wasn't time yet for them to learn, embrace, or possess them. Since the role of mother is ultimately ongoing, you have a multitude of opportunities to impart the skills that may have been overlooked.

I encourage you to take some time to create your own checklist, not to use it as an absolute standard for what you *must* do, but rather as a list of goals you aspire to. And if you hear your internal grading system kicking in, remind yourself of the one basic truth we're speaking about here: THERE IS NO SUCH THING AS A PEFECT MOTHER.

Making Mistakes

Every problem has a gift for you in its hands.   RICHARD BACH

Imagine for a moment that you did it: that you achieved your objective and were crowned *The Perfect Mother*. Whether your role model is Jackie Kennedy Onassis, Donna Reed, or the woman who lives across the street from you, what if you lived up to all your expectations? What if you did everything right? What if you had the foresight to anticipate what buttons your children might push, and you could head them off at the pass? Imagine: peace and tranquility without any flare-ups. Picture your child, clean, neat, beautifully dressed, joyful and happy, grateful and polite. What if you trusted yourself completely, knowing that you couldn't make a mistake, and fear and doubt were never part of the equation? Consider what your life would be like if you were, in fact, the perfect mother.

We know that this is a myth. However, visiting that oasis of harmony probably wasn't so bad. The absence of worry, fear, and anxiety was probably a welcome respite.

But consider the downside. If you were the perfect mother, what could you learn? What would be your challenges? What would your child learn? Would the perfect mother have the perfect child? What lessons could be learned by perfect people? If the point of being human is to learn lessons, it seems as if being perfect defeats the purpose. The concept of perfection does seem to eliminate embarrassment, humiliation, and shame. However, with nothing to learn and no possible opportunities to grow, it could be pretty boring.

You will make mistakes; that's part of the package. There will certainly be moments along the way when you handle situations in ways that you are not proud of, or that you respond to your child in a way that is not the one you would have chosen. The key is not striving to never make any mistakes, but rather handling the ones you do make with humility and a willingness to learn from them.

As I said in *If Life is a Game, These are the Rules*, there are no mistakes, only lessons. Motherhood is a process of trial and error, of journeying from one life stage to the next and accumulating the wisdom available along the way. When your moments of perceived "failure" occur, you are faced with a choice: you can either beat yourself up for it, which only produces more guilt and shame, or you can choose to learn from it, which turns the "mistake" into a valuable lesson.

Rita believed that private school was superior to public school, so she and her husband saved for several years to be able to send their son Tony to a nearby prep school. The summer Tony was 13 years old, they had finally saved enough, and they enrolled him in the private school, beginning the following fall. The only problem was that Tony was happy at his public school and did not want to change schools. He wanted to stay with his friends, his teachers, and the drama club, which he had recently joined. Believing that she knew what was best for her child, Rita insisted that Tony change schools, despite his many protests.

When school started the following September, Tony was miserable. He grew sullen and moped around the house. He missed his friends and was having difficulty fitting in at the new school, where the "cliques" had already formed. His grades suffered and the situation didn't appear to be getting any better as the school year wore on. The tension around the situation escalated, and Rita took Tony to a child psychologist for help, fearing her son was in a real depression.

Ultimately, the psychologist informed Rita that Tony desperately wanted to return to his old school, and that until that happened, Tony's spirits would probably not lift. In a joint session, Tony told Rita he was unhappy that she refused to listen to what he wanted, and that he felt like his wants and needs were unimportant to her. Rita listened with a heavy heart, realizing that in her effort to give her son the education she had never had, she had carelessly overlooked his independent needs. She agreed that Tony could go back to his old school the following fall.

Rita was faced with two options at this point: she could berate herself endlessly for causing her child pain, or she could remember that she was doing the best she could and acting in the way she thought would be best for her child. She chose to forgive herself, knowing her actions were motivated by love. She also apologized to Tony and tried to make amends for what had happened, and ultimately came to see that she needed to consult with Tony about major decisions affecting his daily life whenever it was possible and appropriate. From then on, Rita never dismissed Tony's thoughts or feelings when it came to making choices about his life.

When you make what you perceive to be a "mistake," there are three steps you can take so that the perceived failure can be turned around and put to good use. They are:

1. forgive yourself
2. make it right
3. find the lesson

FORGIVING YOURSELF

It's not easy to forgive yourself when you have behaved in a way you are not proud of, but it is especially hard when that behavior negatively affects your children. It can be heartbreaking to look into their eyes and know you have hurt them, or treated them in any way that is less than honorable.

Forgiveness is the act of erasing an emotional debt. Forgiveness is necessary in order to heal from past incidents. Before you forgive yourself, you will need to open your heart, or in other words, tap into your compassion. By opening your heart, you can find the empathy to make amends with yourself. In this conscious and deliberate act, you absolve and free yourself from guilt and self-recrimination. You can close your eyes and say words of forgiveness. You can write a letter giving yourself a clean slate. You can look in the mirror and tell yourself that you are released from the burden of guilt. You can do whatever it takes to let yourself off the hook.

In the process of forgiving yourself, it helps to remind yourself of two things. First, that you probably did not intend to hurt your child, or cause him any unhappiness. Second, you were most likely doing the best you could with the resources you had at that moment.

Bonnie felt terrible. She lost her temper with her six-year-old son, Mickey, who was upstairs in his room crying as though the world had ended. She hadn't meant to, but she was under deadline pressure and Mickey kept interrupting with questions and demands. She called me in that moment to consult on how she could handle the situation.

"I'm just so disgusted with myself," she said. "I can't believe I snapped at poor Mickey."

"Did you intend to make him feel bad?" I asked gently.

"Of course not!" she responded immediately.

"And can you recognize that you reacted with the limited amount of patience you had at that moment, when you were under stress?" I asked.

"I suppose so."

"Well, the first thing you need to do is let yourself off the hook. That doesn't mean you justify your actions, it just means that you forgive yourself for them. You're not making what you did 'okay,' but you are separating your negative action from your entire perception of your self. One bad moment doesn't make you a bad mother," I said.

I went on to discuss with Bonnie how she could apologize and make the best of the situation. We agreed the Mickey was old enough to be able to understand if Bonnie said she was sorry and explained why she had lost her temper. Once she was able to forgive herself, she could move into action and make amends with her son.

Forgiving yourself takes work, yet it is an essential step in turning a perceived failure into an opportunity for learning and growth.

MAKING IT RIGHT

The second stage involves doing whatever is necessary to make amends for your mistake. It may be apologizing to your child or reversing the decisions that were made in your previous state of mind. It could be altering logistics, changing plans, or reversing momentum to go in another direction. You might even make significant changes in the way you and your child interact.

When you make a situation "right," you in effect undo the wrong that you perceive has been done. If you accused your child of tracking mud into the house and you later found out it was the furniture movers, making amends is definitely in order. If you jumped to conclusions about why your child didn't call when she said she would, and later found out that it was not possible, you want to make it up to her. If you punished your child unreasonably, taking your anger out on her rather than helping her learn something, you probably want to set things straight and release the shame and guilt. Making a situation right involves two people: you and your child.

Making amends can be as simple as saying you are sorry, and as complex as radically changing the way you relate to your child in certain situations. In Penny's case, it was the latter.

Penny remarried five years after she left her husband, who was the father of her 14-year-old daughter, Jessica. She married a man with two kids of his own, and in an effort to make them a happy family unit, she spent a lot of time with her new stepchildren. What she neglected to notice was the effect the new arrangement was having on Jessica. She had become sullen and withdrawn, and her grades started slipping. It wasn't until Jessica almost failed biology that Penny realized something major was up.

Penny and Jessica came to see me, and Jessica revealed that she had felt abandoned and left out ever since the marriage.

"You spend so much time with his kids, it's like you forgot you had one of your own," she said tearfully. "You never pay any attention to me at all! It's like your new family is so much more important than me."

Penny was speechless. She thought she had been doing the right thing by trying to create a new, happy home for Jessica. She had always felt guilty about the divorce, which deprived Jessica of a "normal" family life, and this was her way of trying to make it up to her. As she listened to her heartbroken daughter, she realized with horror that her radar had been way off.

"Jessie, I'm so sorry," she said. "What can I do to make this up to you?"

The three of us then spent the better part of two hours figuring out what it would take for Penny to make amends. The fact that she really heard her daughter and was willing to see things from her perspective went a long way toward advancing the process. From there, we mapped out a schedule so Jessica could have "alone time" with her mother, the way she used to. They created a plan that included all the other family members, so Jessica could be included in their activities with her mother. It took a lot of work, but Jessica and Penny got back on track, as Penny made amends to her daughter for causing her pain.

When you find yourself in a situation in which you need to make amends, ask yourself what it would take to make things right again. If you don't come up with the answer on your own, ask your child. Chances are he or she will be more than happy to tell you.

FINDING THE LESSONS

The last step in handling a "mistake" is to find the lesson for you and/or your child hidden within it. There is only one question you need to ask yourself in order to find the lesson: "What can this situation teach me?"

One word of advice: do not search for the lesson until the emotions of the situation are calmed. If you are in the thick of it, it can be difficult to see it with a cool head and willing eyes. For more ideas on how to find and learn the lessons available to you, refer back to chapter 6.

Dealing with Regrets

One of the things I suggest to mothers to help them get past their regrets is to communicate their thoughts and feelings directly to their child, but only when their child is old enough to understand them as adults.

When my daughter turned eighteen and graduated from high school, I felt a need to say so many things to her, but I couldn't find the words. I wanted to tell her how I felt, what I wanted for her, but even more than that I wanted to let her know my hopes, expectations, fears, and wishes. I wanted her to know the ways I felt I had let her down. Whether my expectations were based on myth or reality, I felt I had to share my truth with her to release myself from the shadow of imperfection and open a new chapter for both of us.

The following is a condensed version of that letter:

Dear Jenn,

As we approach your graduation and your eighteenth birthday, I find myself filled with mixed emotions.

I am happy for you to have achieved this age of adulthood, yet I'm afraid that I haven't done enough—and time is quickly running out. I am sad you are leaving home to go out into the world, yet I know you are ready and it is time. I am eager for you to see the world, to learn and grow, but I am fearful of some of the people you may encounter.

I am excited about the wonderful life you have in front of you, yet I'm concerned about how easily you are influenced by others.

I am proud that you are going to the university, yet I'm anxious about your ability to manage your time, priorities, and projects.

I know that you are beautiful, bright, assertive, strong,

resourceful, articulate, and infinitely capable of achieving anything you set your mind to, yet I wonder if you will utilize your gifts and learn from every experience that happens.

I know you are a terrific person, and deep down I fear I haven't been everything I should have been—that maybe I haven't been the best mom.

I wonder, did I bake enough cookies?

Did I make enough crafts?

Did I read to you enough?

Did I play with you enough?

Did I do enough homework with you?

Did I hold you and cuddle with you enough so that you know forever how much I love you?

Did I spend enough time giving you values that you will have for the rest of your life?

Would I have done it differently? Only if the circumstances had been different.

Do I regret it? No, not really. Do I wish I could do it over? No. But I do dearly hope that after the last eighteen years you know most of all that you are treasured—that there is nothing I wouldn't do for you—that I believe in you and know you have everything you need to make your life everything you want.

You are a star. Not because of me, but because of *you*.

I've made mistakes—and learned lessons—many of them, as you have and will. It will be challenging for both of us to embrace your imperfections, since so much of you is flawless. You will have to deal with forgiving yourself, and I will have to accept disappointment, On the other hand, we will celebrate your successes together and rejoice in your achievements.

It's a time of change, a time of redefining. It's time for creating a new relationship between us—woman to woman.

You will make your own choices now, based on your head, heart, gut, and spirit. It's a time of soul searching and looking in the mirror—

Who do you see? Who do you want to see? What does that person in the mirror want to say to you? What do you truly want in life?

This is a moment of new beginnings—you are launching a life.

I want the world for you—nothing less—and I want, my dearest daughter, for all your dreams to come true.

I love you with all my heart,

Mommy

I gave this letter to Jennifer a few weeks before she left for college. It was my way of sending her off into the world knowing all that I feel for her, and gaining some sense of closure on my experience of raising her from being a tiny baby to the adult she now is. I needed her to know that I may not have been perfect but that I always did the best I could, and that I was proud of who she had become.

You can write a letter to your own child. Your letter will most likely be very different. You will ask forgiveness for different things.

But for you to forgive yourself and absolve yourself for not being the perfect mother, you need to look yourself in the eye and see where you haven't measured up to your own expectations. Where do you feel you have not measured up to your vision of the mother you wanted to be? Where have you let yourself down? When did you let your child down? The more honest you can be with yourself, the sooner you can learn to forgive yourself and move on with a clean slate, knowing you did the best you could at the time. Remember, each day is a new beginning.

My daughter has never judged me as harshly as I have judged myself. She believes I have been and continue to be a terrific mother. Have I been perfect? No. Terrific? Maybe not, but certainly good enough in her eyes. and that's whose opinion really counts!

If you allow yourself to be yourself and do the very best you can, you will be successful as a mother. If you learn from what happens and apply it to the next incident, you will be continuously improving. If you realize that you have influence over your child for a brief moment in time, and you use that power wisely, then you will be practicing the art of motherhood perfectly.

MOTHERHOOD IS A
JOURNEY THAT NEVER ENDS

Children will grow up. However, you remain a parent forever.

$\mathcal{B}$eing a mother is a lifelong journey. Your relationship with your children will change over time, as it should, but once you become a mother, you will always be a mother. You will want the best for your offspring regardless of your age or theirs. You will want them to experience the least amount of pain, sorrow, and hurt. You will want them to have health, long life, joy, fulfillment, and love. You will want them to make the right decisions and avoid those that cause embarrassment, ridicule, and shame. Most of all you will want their ultimate happiness. You never cease being a mother; it is a primary part of your life forever.

As each page of the calendar turns, another adventure lies waiting to greet you. Just when you've figured out how to hold, feed, and burp your newborn and calm him to sleep, your child becomes a toddler and you need to be one step ahead, gating the staircase, safety-proofing the entire house, and providing capped cups that can be held and dropped without spilling. The sting of leaving your child at nursery school that first day quickly becomes a blurred memory as you attempt to juggle peanut butter and jelly sandwiches, soccer games, baby teeth under pillows, and carpools. Swimming and soccer, ballet and basketball practice, piano and piccolo, Scout meetings and youth groups keep you driving around in your car for years. Then it's onto pimples, puberty, and proms. Before you know it, you're videotaping a high school graduation. When your child ventures out into the real world, you're faced with the toughest task of all: letting go.

Getting "There"

When I wrote *If Life is a Game, These are the Rules*, I talked about one of the basic truths of being human: the fact that "there" is no better than "here." When you raise children, there is a real trap in believing that there is a "there" there. There is no "there," for each time you reach "there," you realize you have arrived at yet another "here."

For instance, imagine uttering or thinking any of the following:

"When he stops teething, then life will be easier."

"When he is potty trained, I will feel less constrained."

"When he grows out of the terrible twos, things will be smoother."

"When he starts school, then I will get a break."

"As soon as he gets his driver's license, I will have it easier."

"When he finally graduates, things will be better!"

"Once he gets married, I'll worry about him less."

You can deceive yourself into thinking that all your problems will magically disappear when whatever challenge you are presently dealing with is over. You may promise yourself that motherhood will become the bowl of cherries you thought it would be "as soon as . . ." The reason this myth is so attractive is because there is hope of relief at the end of the process. It makes contentment the light at the end of the tunnel, and would have you defer your well-being and happiness until you arrive there.

Throughout the mothering process, there are definite "there's." Each one resembles an oasis in the middle of the desert. In fact, they are mirages that evaporate when you reach them. The reality is that when you reach "there" it becomes "here," and there is a brand new "there." Somehow it doesn't seem fair. However, it's a very important part of the process. Once you understand the cyclical nature of life, you realize that a viable alternative is choosing to be present here and now, appreciating what you have rather than wishing it were already in the past. If you're not careful, you could end up wishing your child's entire childhood were over. Then when your child was grown, you would nostalgically wish you had it all back to do over again.

Jennifer's graduation from high school was an emotionally tumultuous time. I remember thinking, "When she goes to college, then it will be easier." There I was, stepping into the trap of the future oasis that would provide respite. No sooner had she arrived at college than there were roommate difficulties. Then came sorority rush with its politics and squabbles, and then on to the "freshman fifteen" (pounds accumulated during her first year). Next came sliding grades because of an expanded social life, mounting expenses, and a request for a cell phone to keep up with the other kids. Things had changed once she was no longer living under our roof, but the problems hadn't disappeared—they had just moved 3,000 miles away. I heard about the boyfriend traumas, the betrayal by supposed good friends, and both the terrific and the unfair professors. The main differences were that our phone bill increased, I had far less control than I'd had when she lived at home, and I could no longer take her in my arms and hold her when she wanted her mom. Things were different, not necessarily "easier." My role as a mom had evolved yet again, and there were new triumphs and challenges to deal with. The good news is that she confided in me and told me what was happening, and I still felt I was a part of her life regardless of the distance between us.

The way to escape the "here/there" cycle is to be where you are, when you are there. When you let go of the idea that there is any "there" to reach, you can relax into the process of being where you are at each moment and be present. You can cease wasting time and energy racing toward some point in the future and live each moment and situation as it arises. After all, mothering is an endless series of new experiences, new opportunities to grow, and new lessons in the wonderful school of life. Remember, there is no end to the journey of motherhood.

A woman in one of my seminars told this story:

"When my daughter Sidney was 35, she decided to leave her husband. The marriage had not been good from the start, and I think she made the right decision. She had very little savings, plus my two grandchildren to take care of, and there she was, with nowhere to go. Of course, her dad and I opened our doors and took them right in, but boy, was it a shock! I thought my 'mommy' days were behind me, but when I saw how much my daughter needed me during that time, I realized that I would never stop being 'mommy,' no matter how old Sidney was."

Ideally, your children will only need you in the best of circumstances: to share the joys and the good aspects of their new lives. However, parenting grown children—like parenting little ones—is a mixed bag, and you can never really know what to expect. The only constant you can count on is that your role of "mother" will continuously evolve.

When Your Baby Isn't a Baby Anymore

Does it seem impossible that the child will grow up? That the bashful smile will become a bold expression . . . that a briefcase will replace the blue security blanket? ANN BEATTIE

In some ways, your child will always be your "baby." You will always think of her as your child, even when she has grown into a fully-fledged adult. As she grows, you will continually need to form entirely new relationships with her: ones based on mutual respect, understanding, and ultimately, admiration.

HAVING REALISTIC EXPECTATIONS

One of the challenges of motherhood is having realistic expectations of children. Seeing who they are and what they are capable of is a large part of the process. As they change, as they grow and develop, your expectations must shift also. It is not appropriate to expect a two-year-old to balance her checkbook, just as it is not appropriate to tuck a 30-year-old in bed and read her bedtime stories, unless she has a disability. But things aren't always that obvious. There are times when your child has matured, but you haven't noticed it and are still treating him as you used to. Like the mother who is still cutting her 12-year-old's meat or tells her 16-year-old to be home by 9 P.M., you will have moments when you must wake up and get with the program. This is not to say that you should do everything at the exact time that conventional wisdom dictates. You need to make your own decisions for and with your children, based on their maturity level and level of competence, and taking into consideration their overall safety. You also need to take into account the time and place in which you live.

I attended an all-girls private Catholic school for thirteen years during the 1950s and '60s. Everything was very proper. We wore uniforms, walked in silent ranks from class to class, and curtsied when we addressed an adult. Times were different then. If I expected my daughter to curtsy every time she met an adult, I would be setting up unrealistic expectations. First of all, it wouldn't happen, and second, it would show that I was disconnected from present realities. Just because things were a certain way when I was an adolescent, doesn't mean that they are that way now. For some mothers this may be a wake-up call. Ask yourself these questions:

1. What are my expectations of my child?
2. Are my expectations realistic given his or her age?
3. Are my expectations realistic given where we live?
4. Are my expectations realistic given present cultural norms?
5. What shift do I need to make to see things clearly as they are?

As your children mature, you will be called on to shift your consciousness, focus, and priorities with their development. They are not who they once were. We don't always have rites of passage in every culture to be able to make smooth transitions. It is obvious when your child starts to walk. You can see it, and you realize that you must child-proof the house. Toddlers must have the freedom to move about and use their limbs, and the environment must be safe for them. It is not so obvious how you should balance freedom and safety when your child turns 13, 16, 18, or 20. You may be looking through the same lens you used when they were 10 years old. Things may change right under your nose without your realizing it.

Dawn was 17, but her mother Sandra still treated her as if she were 13. She insisted that Dawn be home on weekend nights by ten, even though most of her friends didn't have to be home until midnight. She didn't allow Dawn to wear any makeup, go on dates, or even wear miniskirts, saying no "respectable" girl would do such things. She thought it was fine for her daughter to do what she wanted once she was 21, but while Dawn was living under her roof, she was expected to obey Sandra's rules.

While every mother has a right to raise her daughter however she sees fit, there are instances where a mother's refusal to "get with the times" can cause undue stress on their relationship and on her child's social life. It doesn't hurt to take a look around every now and then for a reality check, to see if perhaps you might be out of sync with what other kids your child's age are doing today. Once you have that information, you can make a more informed choice about what you allow your own child to do.

In Sandra and Dawn's case, the situation grew so strained that they came to see me together. I gave them each an exercise: I told Dawn to go out and interview five mothers of girls her age to see what they allowed their daughters to do. I told Sandra to interview five girls Dawn's age to see what their lives were like and what they were doing regarding curfews, makeup, boys, etc. Both did their assignments, and both were surprised by the results. Dawn was surprised to see that most of the mothers weren't as lenient as she had assumed they were, and Sandra discovered that being a 17-year-old these days was very different from when she was that age. She also saw that she had been treating Dawn more like a 13-year-old than a mature young woman almost ready to graduate high school. From there, they were able to negotiate new rules that both were comfortable with.

Allowing them to make their own choices

As your children grow up, you will be needed in many different ways. Sometimes they will need you for advice on practical matters, such as financial arrangements, career decisions, or even how to make spaghetti. They will also, at times, need you to step back and allow them to live their lives in their own way.

Your children grow into young adults, and suddenly you see them struggling to find their way. You watch their loves come and go. You want them to make the right choices . . . yet you stay at arm's length to let them learn their own lessons. You observe them being hired for various jobs, and you wish and hope for the best. They may be downsized, promoted, or passed over. Regardless, you stand in the wings of their lives, wanting only the best for them, trying somehow to shield them from harm, pain, and even from their own errors. However, you cannot shield them forever. You must let them learn from adversity, from repetition, and from failure. You cannot shield them from failure, for some of the greatest learning in life comes from adversity and defeat. If they never faltered, they would never appreciate the triumph of a breakthrough. If they never suffered, they would not cherish joy and pleasure. If they never failed, they wouldn't savor the sweet taste of victory. It is in growing that the lessons are learned. After all, there is not much that can be learned from doing everything perfectly. It is personal triumph in overcoming adversity, hardship, and obstacles that builds character.

You may see them making life choices that give you pause, as in Angelina's case. Angelina had eight children. As they reached maturity, they chose mates and started families—all except her second son,

Antonio. Antonio passed through his teens and twenties and on into his thirties before finding a woman whom he brought home to meet her. Angelina was shocked. The woman didn't match her mental picture of whom Antonio would marry. She was very strong, dominant, and older than he was; she had two children and was an accomplished physician. Angelina had serious doubts that they would choose to have more children together. Every time Angelina saw Liz, she shuddered. It was painful to imagine Antonio with someone so different from the woman she imagined her son would marry.

One day Antonio came to his mother and said, "I love Liz, and I want your blessing." It was a moment of truth, and Angelina struggled with her answer.

"Are you sure, son?"

"Mother, she is the most wonderful woman in the world. Don't you see how much like you she is?"

"Really, you think so?"

"She is strong like you. She knows her own mind like you. She is focused just like you are. She is loving, kind, and fun just like you, Mom."

Angelina stood there shocked that her son saw her this way and that Liz reminded him of her. She started to laugh. He asked her what was so funny. She said, "I wanted a nice, young, sweet girl for you, but that's not what *you* want."

"I wouldn't be interested in that kind of girl. You have been the best mother to me because you have shown me exactly the type of wife I want—one who has your qualities. I know this marriage will work out because I feel so at home with her."

Angelina had to let go. She had to let go of believing that only she knew what was right for her son. She had to let go of the distance she had created between Liz and herself.

Your child's path in life may be a hot spot. You may have an idea in your mind of the profession, vocation, or life pursuit that is reasonable, right, or appropriate, but it may not match your child's. Your child may choose to be a doctor or a painter, or to join the Peace Corps. She may decide to work in a city near you or relocate thousands of miles away. She may choose to get married and live a traditional lifestyle, or choose an alternative route. Either way, it is ultimately her choice, not yours. You can be there for discussion and input if asked, for your thoughts and feelings when appropriate. But if you try to impose your vision, you may be disappointed with the results.

Audrey was thrilled about her daughter's upcoming marriage to Mark, whom she considered the perfect young man for Alley. Audrey was busy with all the plans—the flowers, the table arrangements, the music, the food, all the details to create the perfect day for her daughter. I met with Alley and Mark, who had asked if I would officiate at their ceremony. I agreed and we discussed the sequence of events. At one point, Alley confided in me that Audrey was driving her crazy. I asked what she was doing, and I got an earful.

"She is a carrier of anxiety. We're getting so uptight that it's all becoming work. We've stopped having fun."

"What is she focused on?"

"The latest is that she wants me to wear high heels," Alley said.

"You don't want to, I take it," I commented.

"No, I want to wear tennis shoes so I'm comfortable. Besides, with the length of my gown no one will ever see them," Alley stated.

I saw my opening. "Remember, you two, this is your day. Your mother has had her day. This day is all about the two of you, your union, and the beginning of your life together. This is the official acknowledgment and celebration of your love for each other and the public declaration of it. Tell your mother that you are wearing whatever shoes you want to, and she doesn't need to concern herself with that item," I proposed.

They both thanked me for clarifying the purpose of their wedding, and from there on in things went quite smoothly. Alley did wear her bridal tennis shoes, no one noticed, and she was comfortable and happy.

When your children start their own families

It can sometimes be difficult to accept the fact that when your children grow up and get married, they have formed new families of their own. Hopefully, you are still very much a part of their lives, but you are no longer their only family, and thus not as central. I've seen this frequently with mothers who have difficulty allowing their sons' wives to replace them as the primary woman in their lives. One woman I consulted told me that it took her four years to get her new mother-in-law to stop buying her husband's underwear!

Carolyn's granddaughter was born with a respiratory problem. The doctors weren't sure if the baby would live. Carolyn was so heavily involved in the situation that Glen, her son-in-law, felt eclipsed by her. Her daughter Sue was so involved with the baby—

and with her mother—that she was ignoring her husband. "After all," Sue rationalized, "my mother has raised four children, and Glen is dealing with his first." Glen was feeling left out. He wanted to face the situation together with his wife and not be pushed aside by mother and daughter. The situation finally came to a head one day when Glen exploded at Carolyn, "Why don't you let Sue and me handle this?! After all, this is our baby." Carolyn left the house hurt and wounded. The situation was unfortunate; the closeness between mother and daughter had excluded the baby's father from the discussions.

Things did get patched up, and Carolyn realized that she had been overstepping her bounds. She was more sensitive in the future and deliberately encouraged Glen and Sue to build their family and make their own decisions together. A mother's real opportunity at this stage is to offer support let her child learn life's lessons, and be there when asked, remaining sensitive to the new family dynamic.

When your children start their own families, it's important for you to remember that they are the ones in the parent role with regard to their children, not you. The good news is that now you get to be a grandparent, which means you get all the delicious benefits of the children, and none of the direct responsibility!

The torch has been passed. Whereas you once went from "maiden" to "mother," you now graduate to the most advanced level of mother, "grandmother." You go from teacher to provider of wisdom, from knowledgeable to sagacious, authority to overseer. Revel in your new role, for now your children are using the mothering you gave them to raise their own children. What a blessing!

Letting Go

A mother is not a person to lean on but a person to make leaning unnecessary.   DOROTHY CANFIELD FISHER

One of the greatest ironies of parenting is that you put all this time, energy, and effort into raising your children, only to have them eventually fly from the nest and leave you. That's the fate of a mother: to give, to nurture, to guide, to teach, and then, ultimately, to let go.

There are so many points along the way when letting go is the greatest expression of love you can give your children. From the moment they wave good-bye their first day of kindergarten to the moment they walk down the aisle at their wedding, your heart will probably never get used to the pang of seeing them spread their wings and start to take flight. Part of you may always secretly wish that they might continue to need you even just a little tiny bit, to rely on you as a source of support in life. Simultaneously, another part of you knows deep down that their self-sufficiency and independence are what everything you have ever done for them was really about.

While the most challenging part of raising children is officially complete when they leave the house, letting go doesn't mean that they won't be back. They will return to share more triumphs and woes, to connect with the one who gave them life, and to give back to you who so selflessly gave everything to them. If you have done your job well, then you will see a happy, fulfilled, young adult who is growing, learning, contributing to the community, and participating in your family in new and mature ways.

Every year at Thanksgiving, Marsha's three daughters would "help" prepare the meal. When they were small, Marsha would let them mash the potatoes in a big bowl on the floor. Usually they would end up with more potatoes in their hair than in the bowl, but it was fun nonetheless. When they got a little older, two of them learned to bake, and they would make terrific "secret recipe" desserts for the family for Thanksgiving. It was sad for Marsha when her daughters married and moved away, and she had trouble relinquishing her vision of the family all together for her favorite holiday. She didn't know if Thanksgiving would ever be the same again, but she did know that it was time for her to let go and allow the girls to make their own choices about where they would spend the holidays.

But what Marsha didn't count on was how strongly the seeds of tradition she planted had taken root for her daughters. Every year, all three women return home for Thanksgiving with their new families in tow. And now it is her grandchildren who mash the potatoes in the big bowl on the floor, still with more in their hair than anywhere near the bowl. And cleaning up the mess makes Marsha as happy as anything she does all year.

You have given them roots, and wings. You provided the framework for them to grow in a healthy manner. You provided the nest from which they could launch their flight into the world. You are indeed the wind beneath their wings. Your nest will always be there for them to return to. Your wind will always be there to support their safe flight. None of that will ever change. And when they need that gentle, supportive, caring mom to work her magic with their own little ones, you will be there again with wide open arms. Each new challenge is yet another opportunity to bring the two of you together to laugh, to share, to solve problems, and to learn from and with each other. One day you will have the opportunity to reverse roles. The ones you raised will then be able to care for you as you once cared for them.

Letting go is necessary and can be painful at times. When to let go and to what degree are critical questions that require some inner work. After you've read books on pregnancy, parenting, and motherhood, you must turn within and seek inner wisdom to guide your choices, and to know how and when it is time to let go.

How to let go

Letting go is a gradual process. It doesn't happen in your sleep, or with the close of a door. It happens by degrees, slowly, in your own time, at your own pace, and only when you are ready. In order to let go, you must prepare yourself on three levels: mentally, spiritually, and emotionally.

Mental preparation involves logic and rational thought. When you prepare mentally, you imagine why letting go makes sense. You have conversations with yourself that explain and justify your choice. You analyze the process and you try to make sense out of the situation.

Spiritual preparation means connecting with the big picture, the larger context. When you prepare spiritually, you connect with your spirit and your higher self to seek the right course of action for everyone involved. When you prepare spiritually you use prayer, meditation, and moments of quiet reflection to receive guidance from whatever higher source you draw from.

Emotional preparation means processing the feelings associated with the situation. The more you want to hold on, the more painful the process of letting go becomes. Holding on means that you are afraid to trust yourself, your child, the situation, and perhaps even God. The feelings associated with letting go can be loss, sadness, fear, and pain. When you process these feelings, you allow yourself to experience the full range of emotions and let them pass through you. You don't hold back, repress, or act stoical, but rather purge your feelings in order to cleanse and release them, to clear out the past and open the door for the future.

When you effectively let go, you make a statement in good faith to the universe that you:

- Trust the situation, and all involved
- Believe that you have done an adequate job
- Know that there are lessons your child must learn on his or her own
- Have confidence in your child's ability to successfully handle challenges

When Jennifer graduated from high school, she left for Europe with her best friend. The trip was a gift from her family to commemorate her eighteenth birthday, her graduation, and her entry into the adult world. It was the first time she had traveled without an adult accompanying her. I had many concerns based on her childhood experiences. I was nervous that she might lose her plane tickets, passport, Europass, or money. I was concerned that she might have some of her possessions stolen from her. I was worried that she might hurt herself. I was afraid that she might meet people who would take advantage of her, that something terrible might happen.

Intellectually, I dealt with logistics. I gave her names of friends in every country whom she could contact for lodging, and help, and in case of emergencies. I gave her travelers' cheques and a credit card just in case she needed it. I bought her a backpack, walking shoes, and equipment so she could travel light and keep track of her possessions. I told myself how resourceful she had always been and convinced myself that she was infinitely capable of handling most situations. I addressed my fears through strategy, planning, and self-talk.

On the spiritual side, I prayed to stop worrying, to be able to trust that everything would be all right. Whenever I became anxious, I turned to my spirit to guide my compass in the higher realms.

On the emotional side, I was just afraid to let go. I was scared that something negative might happen, and I would be responsible and to blame for letting her go. I had to feel the fear and then go deep within myself to find the trust to support my choice.

Jennifer went on her trip. It lasted three weeks, and she had a terrific time. Nothing adverse happened, and both girls learned and grew from being on their own for the first time. It was a learning process for everyone involved. I probably should have been clearer about the definition of "emergency," as her credit card use showed that her definition was different from mine. However, in the process of letting go, I allowed Jennifer to find her wings and take flight.

Letting go and trusting your child to go out into the world ultimately means trusting yourself. It means trusting that you've done the right thing—that you have provided the values, the love, the structure, the guidance in making wise choices, and the role modeling to show them the way. You have done the best you could, and chances are you have done an even better job than you think you have. When you reach the precipice and it's time to let go, there's nothing to do but take a deep breath, reaffirm your trust in the universe, and make the leap. Where you'll land is the next great mystery on your path as a mother!

After your children are grown and gone, there comes a moment when you realize your life is radically different from the way it has been for the past two decades. The hallways of your home no longer echo with children's laughter or piercing screeches of "Mom!" Where before your dinner table was bustling and busy, now it's just you and your spouse, continuing on with the next phase of your life's journey.

You will always be a mother. With every breath you take, you will know your children are out there somewhere, hopefully living the best lives they can. They will always be in the corner of your mind, and in the center of your heart. Though they may not need you to bandage their scratches or set boundaries with their social life, they will need you in other ways: ways you will continue to discover as you journey forth into the next phase of motherhood, and the next, forever more.

Blessings to you on your journey!

Dear Mother,

Whether you have chosen to have a child, or you are a new mother, or you have raised children and grandchildren, you have the experience of being committed to those you dearly love. *The Gift of Motherhood: 10 Truths for Every Mother* has been written for you. It presents the universal principles that guide motherhood. It is to be used as your companion as you mother your child. Use it as a reference book as you evolve through each phase. Refer to it when you have questions or if you are confused, uncertain, or fearful. Use it for comfort when you seek reassurance, or use it to reminisce.

The dream of every mother is to have an adult child who is self-confident and considerate, strong yet compassionate, resourceful and reflective. The dream includes being able to meet life's challenges, to learn from them, and to be able to move on and be happy. Throughout all the years of traditional family, single-parenting, blended family, and now empty-nesters, there is confusion, doubt, uncertainty, and fear that the dream will ever become a reality. It is heart-warming and gratifying to receive a letter that renounces the fears and confirms the dream. I share Jennifer's letter with you here:

Mommy,

Lately, I have taken some introspective time and I have been journaling.

It's been awhile since I took the time to think about my actions.

Thank you for what you've done.

Thank you for what and who you've made me become.

I've realized that you prepared me a lot better than most of the kids at college. Everyday my adoration and admiration for you grows.

You are the poster on my wall; you are Wonder Woman and I can't tell you how proud I am to call you my mother.

I know that both of our lives don't always allow us to talk as much as we'd like but to be honest we really don't have to.

You are my sunshine and I see you and talk to you at every class, at every meal.

I think of you and I know that that is also true for you. You are the best!

I don't know how anyone could ever compare to the mother that God gave me. I have never-ending pride about your accomplishments, your strength, and your beauty.

You are my biggest hero and I am your biggest fan.

Although we are hundreds of miles apart you are very much a part of me.

There is nothing for me to revolt against. You have given me an identity in which to grow . . . with and from.

I can't tell you how much you are a gift in my life.

I could have never made it without you.

You make me proud to be your daughter.

I love you.
Jenn

May you receive in every form available the sentiments expressed in this letter from your daughter or son and come to realize that doing your best was good enough. May you forgive all your shortcomings and discover that you have raised an adult child who can create a life filled with happiness, fulfillment, and love.

If the principles in this book resonate with you, and you want more morsels of universal wisdom, you are invited to continue your spiritual development through our workshops, trainings, personalized coaching, and my other books.

I wish you the fulfillment of all your dreams, especially with your children and in everything you do.

Chérie Carter-Scott, Ph.D.

Resources

Books

Birthing from Within by Pam England and Rob Horowitz. Albuquerque: Partera Press, 1998.

Chicken Soup for the Expectant Mother's Soul by Jack Canfield, Mark Victor Hansen, Patty Aubery, and Nancy Mitchell Autio. Deerfield Beach: Health Communications, 2000.

Chicken Soup for the Mother's Soul by Jack Canfield, Mark Victor Hansen, Marci Shimoff, and Jennifer Read Hawthorne. Deerfield Beach: Health Communications, 1997.

The Child with Special Needs by Stanley I. Greenspan, M.D. and Serena Wieder, Ph.D. Cambridge: Perseus Press, 1998.

Children Learn What They Live: Parenting to Inspire Values by Dorothy Law Nolte. New York: Workman Publishing, 1998.

The Complete Book of Pregnancy and Childbirth by Sheila Kitzinger. New York: Knopf, 1996.

Complete Guide to Pediatric Symptoms, Illnesses & Medications by H. Winter Griffith. Thousand Oaks: H.P. Books, 1989.

The Eight Seasons of Parenthood by Barbara C. Uncell and Jerry L. Wyckoff, Ph.D. New York: Crown, 2001.

Everyday Blessings by Myla and Jon Kabat-Zinn. New York: Hyperion, 1998.

Guide to Your Child's Nutrition by American Academy of Pediatrics, William H. Dietz and Lorain Stern, Eds. New York: Villard, 1999.

If High School is a Game, Here's How to Break the Rules by Chérie Carter-Scott, Ph.D. New York: Random House, 2001.

In Praise of Single Parents by Shoshana Alexander. Boston: Houghton Mifflin Co., 1994.

Inner View: A Woman's Daily Journal by Chérie Carter-Scott, Ph.D., Diana Lynn Schwarzbein, M.D. Santa Barbara: Millenium Press, 1996.

Kids & Money by Jayne A. Pearl. Princeton: Bloomberg Press, 1999.

Magic Trees of the Mind by Marian Diamond and Janet Hopson. New York: Penguin, 1999.

Me, Myself and I by Kyle D. Pruett, M.D. Lanham: Goddard Press, 1999.

Mom, Inc. by Neale S. Godfrey, Tad Richards. New York: Simon & Schuster, 1999.

The Mother's Almanac by Marguerite Kelly and Elia Parsons. New York: Doubleday, 1975.

No Greater Love by Loren Slocum. New York: Golden Books Publishing, 1999.

Parenting Teens with Love and Logic by Foster Cline, M.D. and Jim Fay. Colorado Springs: Navpress, 1993.

The Parents Tao Te Ching by William Martin. New York: Marlowe & Co., 1999.

Raising Lifelong Learners by Lucy Calkins, Lydia Bellino. Cambridge: Perseus Press, 1998.

Step-by-Step Parenting by James D. Eckler. Cincinnati: Betterway Publications, 1993.

10 Principles for Spiritual Parenting by Mimi Doe Walch with Marsha Fayfield Walch. New York: HarperPerennial Library, 1998.

The Unofficial Guide to Having a Baby by Ann Douglas and John R. Sussman, M.D. New York: Hungry Minds, 1999.

What to Expect the First Year by Arlene Eisenberg, Heidi E. Murkoff, and Sandee E. Hathaway. New York: Workman Publishing, 1996.

What to Expect the Toddler Years by Arlene Eisenberg, Heidi E. Murkoff, and Sandee E. Hathaway. New York: Workman Publishing, 1996.

What to Expect When You're Expecting by Arlene Eisenberg, Heidi E. Murkoff, and Sandee E. Hathaway. New York: Workman Publishing, 1996.

YogaBaby by DeAnsin Goodson Parker, Ph.D., Karen W. Bressler. New York: Broadway Books, 2000.

You Are Your Child's First Teacher by Rahima Baldwin Dancy. Berkeley: Celestial Arts, 1989.
Your Baby's Mind by Dr. S. H. Jacob. Avon: Adams Media Corporation, 1992.

Websites

www.abcparenting.com This site contains general information about parenting.

www.about.com This great website allows you to search for ANY topic (e.g., parenting, motherhood, self-esteem, health . . .).

www.csun.edu/~vcpsy00h/parenthood/weblinks.htm California State University, Northridge, offers links to websites they recommend for parents.

www.gymboree.com A site to Gymboree play and music classes offered across the country to children up to four years old.

www.healthatoz.com/atoz/centers/parenting/parindex.asp A site dedicated to healthy children.

www.iparenting.com A wealth of information about parenting!

www.kindermusik.com A site to Kindermusik music and movement classes offered across the country to children up to seven years old.

www.100topparentingsites.com This resource gives you a list of the top 100 parenting sites with direct links to all of them.

www.parenthoodweb.com This resource combines general parenting information along with a calendar of events for parent and/or child activities in your local area.

www.parenting.com A great site to read articles from *Parenting, Baby Talk*, and *Family Life* magazines.

www.parentsoup.com This site has *all* parenting resources in one place!

www.tnpc.com The National Parenting Center gives their "Seal of Approval" (or not) on products and services.

About the Author

New York Times #1 bestselling author Chérie Carter-Scott, Ph.D., has been coaching change successfully for over twenty-eight years. Dr. Carter-Scott is an international author, entrepreneur, consultant, lecturer, teacher/trainer, talk-show host, and seminar leader. Her company, Motivation Management Service Institute, Inc. (MMS), has reached millions of people worldwide. Some of her Fortune 500 corporate clients include FMC, American Express, IBM, GTE, State Farm Insurance, Burger King, and *Better Homes and Gardens* magazine.

Dr. Carter-Scott has promoted her books on numerous media tours around the world, including appearances on several national programs, such as *The Oprah Winfrey Show, Leeza, Politically Incorrect, Sally Jesse Raphael, Jenny Jones,* CNN, and over 500 television and radio talk shows.

Her *New York Times* #1 bestselling book, *If Life is a Game, These are the Rules: Ten Rules for Being Human* was published in September 1998 in twenty-seven countries. Following her appearance on *The Oprah Winfrey Show,* Chérie's book sold over a half a million copies in the first six weeks, selling out every major book seller in the United States. Other national bestseller list rankings include #1 with the *Los Angeles Times* and #1 with major online media source, Amazon.com. Chérie has continued her success with the game-rules series of books with *If Love is a Game, These are the Rules, If Success is a Game, These are the Rules,* and *If High School is a Game, Here's How to Break the Rules.* In addition, Chérie is coauthoring *Chicken*

Soup for the Global Soul with Jack Canfield and Mark Victor Hansen to be released in 2003.

Dr. Carter-Scott has several other published titles: *Negaholics: How to Overcome Negativity and Turn Your Life Around,* which has sold over 100,000 copies; *The Corporate Negaholic: How to Successfully Deal with Negative Employees, Managers and Corporations;* in addition to two self-published books, *The New Species: The Evolution of the Human Being* and *The Inner View: A Woman's Daily Journal.*

She is married and lives in Nevada with her husband and her college-age daughter, Jennifer.